BRITAIN'S PLACE IN THE GREAT PLAN

BY

ANNIE BESANT

Four Lectures delivered in London
June and July 1921

A Yesterday's World Publishing

Published by A Yesterday's World Publishing
Copyright © 2025 A Yesterday's World Publishing
First impression 2025
ISBN - 978-1-916923-49-2

Contents

Lecture I
The Inner Government of the World, or the Power that makes for Righteousness

FRIENDS: In trying to place before you in the four lectures, of which this evening's is the first, a complicated question, largely practical in its outcome, but based on a theory of life and action which underlies and governs the whole of what I have to say, in thinking over that subject, in thinking how I might best present it, since in many of its aspects it is probably unfamiliar to many of you, I thought that I would use the first and second of the lectures more for speaking on the theory than on the practice. Then, having erected a basis from which we might act, I propose to pass on to that question of questions for the World of to-day: Is it possible to reconstruct—in order that mankind may live more nobly and more happily than it does to-day—is it possible to construct a higher, a greater, a more enduring civilisation, because based in accord with the laws amid which we live, so that they shall sustain and support it instead of breaking it into pieces? For, looking back on the many civilisations, ruined one after another, we must, if we think at all of human happiness, we must enquire what was there in those civilisations which brought them to uttermost ruin, and which caused them to disappear? And those of us who believe that Nature is a realm of inviolable law, those of us who believe that all that is against law must perish, and only that which is in accord with it can survive, we naturally seek to find out whether there was something in the past which destroyed those mighty civilisations, whether we can discern any principles for the future which will enable us to erect a civilisation that shall endure; and that is evidently a matter that requires thought and study—study of the past; study of the laws of human society; search after the causes which have brought so many civilisations to their wrecking. And thus thinking, it seems as though we must find some theory of human civilisation, some theory of society, which shall have in it greater elements of permanence than those of the past have shown. That if it be true that evolution is working out, stage after stage, then there may be hope for the future out of the blunders of the past, that we may be able to avoid the rocks on which they were wrecked; for it is, I think, true—a phrase that I have often used— that the map of the past is really the chart of the future; by understanding the mistakes of the past we may avoid them; and so if indeed it be true, as I believe it is, nay, I would dare to say, as I know it is, that there is a Power that makes for Righteousness, that there is an Inner Government of our World—if that be true, the future, despite the clouds of the present, shines with a glory that promises a dawning day. And so in the last two lectures I shall hope to deal more directly with those possibilities of reconstruction than I propose to do in the two first. For it is of no use to talk about Britain's Place in the Great Plan unless we have some conception, however imperfect, of that Plan; and I presume that the question of many who saw the title has been: What is the Great Plan? Is there a Plan at all? For, looking around the world in its present welter, in its present confusion, in its conflicts, its upheavals, its mental and moral earthquakes, can we trace amid that confusion any outline of a Plan which in the future shall be carried out, as the earlier parts of it have to some extent been carried out in the past? For unless we believe that there is a Plan, unless we have caught glimpses of the outline of such a Plan, then we cannot speak about Britain's place in that or any other possible reconstruction; and I want, if I can, to lead you to what is really a great hope for the world—that out of all the sorrow and the blundering, and the misery, and the helplessness apparently of the present, there is a certainty of a greater life extending into an ordered human society, where men shall love instead of hate, where they shall serve each other instead of struggling against each other, where they shall co-operate for a common good, for a common end, and where there shall be a recognition that the duty to the larger self overbears the claims that the smaller selves sometimes make. It is at that that I shall aim.

But I shall be obliged this evening, in the opening up of the subject, to ask you to travel with me into a region which to some of you may seem cloudy and obscure; and yet it is only by some glimpse of that that we can really hope to solve the problems of our present time. Only by some recognition of the laws around us, some understanding of the forces that play about us, may we hope to do what Science has done in the lower physical world; to find out that to live in a realm of law is not a bondage, but a freedom; that it is not a limitation of power, but an increase of power; that as we know the laws, as we understand their working, as we realise the directions in which they tend, they become our servants and not our masters; so that Nature, as has been nobly said, "is conquered by obedience". But while there has been much research into the laws of the physical world, whilst Science has gone far, and sought splendidly, and thought deeply and highly, and so has brought us knowledge of the conditions of the material universe, there has been little recognition of a similar realm of law in the region of the emotions, in the region of the mind; little recognition that society has laws as well as have bodies; that the social union is a thing of law, as well as unions in chemistry or any other science that you may study; and that the same is true there as everywhere—that the more you know of law the more you can use it to bring about the results that you desire. The more you understand its working, the better can you balance one law against another, can neutralise laws which are opposing the working out of your will, laws which prevent your reaching your goal; that so, by such a balancing of laws that are apparently hostile, you may utilise laws that are with you, which will carry you swiftly to your desired object. For it is knowledge that is the master of Nature, whether in the society of human beings or in the lower realms of life, and it is to that idea that I want to lead you.

For that purpose we have to try to find out something of the general outline of our universe, something of those deeper things with which philosophers and metaphysicians deal, the most real of all things because they are nearest to the Life; the most instructive of all things, because they dive most deeply and soar most highly. For men walking about amid the events that are happening in our world are very much like people who wander about the streets of a city not knowing their way, who find themselves in a road, a circus, an alley, and do not know of any plan on which that city is built. And yet if you go up above, up in an aeroplane, you are able to look down and recognise the plan of a well-planned city. You can see from above how to avoid all the obstructions that limited you when you were on a level with them; and so we must be able to take to some extent a mental aeroplane, if we would catch some glimpse of the world as an ordered whole, part of a larger system, and that in turn part of larger and larger systems ever, and yet One Life pervading all, one great Thought working itself out, to be studied in the small in our own world, but to be recognised as having its roots in a vaster world than ours. Otherwise problems will arise that we must put aside as entirely insoluble. How often is it that the astronomer in his study of the vast fields of space finds some motion he does not understand, finds some deviation that he is unable to explain, and then speaks of some force embodied outside the realm of his observation, which may yet be presumed by the intellect to exist because of the results which it shows in the narrower field of his working? And so it is that our astronomers have done much to widen out our field of thought, have corrected many an error which we should have made in the study of our own world alone. They taught us how our sun to us is stationary, and yet is itself moving in a mightier oval in what to us is illimitable space, and how this solar system of ours is but as a sand on the seashore of other systems, and how many of these move round a larger sun, which in its turn again moves round yet a mightier monarch in space, and so on and on and on until none can limit the thinking; facts have to be presumed, where the senses, aided however they may be by apparatus, fail to pierce. And it seems to me that that has done us, that unchallengeable astronomical idea has done us, a great service in studying our own smaller world and our own humanity. For it has helped us to understand that many of those climbing thoughts of spiritual geniuses who have given us the scriptures and the religions of the world, that they have not fallen behind the astronomers in their realisation of the vastness of all that is. And so when we begin to wonder and to speculate, a great idea dawns on the mind of the thinker that Time and Space are really localised, and that the truth lies in what is called, and rightly called, "THE ETERNAL NOW". That there is a region of life in which all exists at every moment of what we call "Time". That there is the One Great Life, full of all possibilities, all actualities, of all that we say has been, is, and shall be; all a mighty fullness; all existing simultaneously; no past, no present, and no future, but the "Now" of an Eternal Life. We confuse our thought when we use that great word "Eternal" as though it were equivalent with "everlasting". Everlasting is of time, but Eternity is outside Time. You in your innermost being are Eternal, part of that Eternal Life out of which are manifested from time to time a universe, a thousand universes, what you will! And that which is simultaneous in the Eternal is successive in the manifestation in which all is limited. And so in the greatest philosophies of the world, whether you take the great Vedânta of the Hindu or whether you take the equally wonderful philosophy of the Mussulman Doctors of the Middle Ages in Europe, you find identity of thought, identity of expression, no possibility of dispute among those whose intellect is able to grasp the problem to some extent, but the bodying out in words, however imperfect, of the same immense thought of the All-pervading and Eternal Life. And in the smaller things around us you will never be able to grasp that great law, called the law of causation, which has become familiar now as Karma; you will never be able to grasp the workings of that law—how it affects the individual how it affects the nation, how it affects humanity—until you realise that in the Eternal everything is interrelated, and that in manifestation all that comes forth is linked together, but in succession, and we speak of past and future. Does it seem an absurdity? I think not, for 1 saw it the other day in an English publication, the record of a scientific society, an idea that I had not before come across in the West—it is more familiar in the East, and may have been long in the West, simply my own lack of knowledge making me not recognise it as western—I saw the suggestion thrown out that the future influences the past. I know it sounds upside down at first sight, and yet it is not so difficult to realise if you think it out. You are all willing to admit that the present is the result of the past. Does it seem a dream, the empty dream of a dreamer, that the future also influences the present, and that the shaping of the present is largely moulded by that which in the future will occur? Think for a moment and you will realise—it is a somewhat coarse illustration from physical nature—that if you have an acorn dropped in the soil, you recognise it, as the fruit of the oak tree, but you know that that acorn can develop into nothing save an oak. It cannot develop into a fish, a bird, or even any other kind of vegetable growth. That which it is to be in the future influences and shapes and guides the growth of that acorn into the tree, because in truth it is not the form that creates the thought, it is the thought that creates the form. Thinking is the one great creative force in our universe; whether it be divine thinking or human thinking, all creations come out of the thought. The sculptor's ideal governs every touch of his fingers on the plastic clay. He has thought the ideal statue before the clay can be moulded or the marble can be carved, and it is this ideal of the sculptor, the thought in his mind, that controls every touch, whether it be of finger or of chisel, and shapes or chips away the super-incumbent material so that the ideal may come out of the marble perfect in all its beauty. And do you realise that that which is here below as to the relation of thought and creation, that that is also so in loftier realms, that everyone of you manifests your Eternal Self, that everyone of you is a fragment of divinity, as each of you is? Do you realise that, in that "far-off" region of spiritual life, where there is no separation but the fragment is inseparate from the whole of which it is a part, that in that mighty world of Spirit you made your own ideal as to your own perfection, you shaped your own thought as to what in your perfection hereafter you would be, and that all through your long incarnation, all down the long string of lives through which you, the Eternal Fragment, are travelling in space and time, and in body after body, it is that Fragment of Divinity that created his ideal, who is striving to shape you, striving to influence you, striving to move you to the nobler and hold you back from the baser, striving for greater power over the lower worlds? He is gaining more and more power, more and more capacity, to guide and rule the matter that he has appropriated for his own purposes, in order that matter may become spiritualised and be a perfect instrument of the unfolded Spirit. Do you realise the possibility that that glory of the future is as real a force as your inheritance of the past, and that the Power in yourself that makes for Righteousness, the hidden God within you, is ever endeavouring to bring about the realisation of his ideal, the ideal which exists in the Eternal, and is still in what we call the future, which is ever reacting upon you in what you call the present, in order that your path may be rightly trodden, may be pursued rightly to its splendid end? At least it is an inspiring thought, a thought that helps us in moments of depression. Did I say depression? There is no depression for him who strives to live in the Eternal, but an abiding peace amid all the storms of time for there is nothing that can shake the Spirit that knows whence he came and whither he goes. Once realise, once reach Self-realisation, and although you may have many more struggles to meet, you know that the end is sure. And looking thus on this large outline, we then try to see—coming down and down and down through many rungs of this mighty ladder which is the manifested Life of the universe, we come down to our own solar system—whether there may be some chance of our finding traces of a Plan. We cannot reach the others, they are far beyond us. But in our own solar system there are certain sources of knowledge available. One, the scriptures of the great religions of the world. They give us broad outlines of the past, the present, and the future. I do not know how far you are aware that in some of the sacred books of the East you find sketches of the future, recognisable sketches of the present that you are able to examine and test. And so it may be worth while sometimes to realise that men have climbed so far, that they have reached a light in which they can see further than we are seeing, and forecast with the sure spiritual vision many of the changes through which our world and our civilisations have passed, or will pass. And after that you come to the traditions of the nations ; and these traditions have been very largely confirmed in our own time by archeological research, which has enormously widened the ordinary educated man's view of the past of the world and the past of humanity, and the various phases through which the races of mankind have gone. And then you can verify some of the smaller of the things and work on a rational hypothesis, even if you feel you cannot take it as anything more. And there is one term upon which for a moment I will pause.

Let us think of Him who is spoken of by the Greeks as the LOGOS, the manifested Word, remembering that in saying "Word" we presuppose that which the Word expresses. And I think there is no better word than that of LOGOS for the Lord of a Universe, since each universe is a fresh expression of divine thought. And so we who are Theosophists use that word in connection with our solar system, and we speak of the SOLAR LOGOS, meaning by that the Lord of our solar universe, our solar system—a universe to us.

There is a verse you may recall out of the old Hebrew writings, where it is said, alluding to what was then called the creation of the world: "When the Morning Stars sang together and all the Sons of God shouted for joy." For a new emanation from the LIFE is a matter of joy, of delight, to those greater Beings who know the outcome of that which then is brought to birth. So that the coming of a universe is rejoiced over by those elder Sons of God; and many a one in reading that verse must have felt startled and wondered who they were, these Sons of God shouting for joy over a world, a system, which, in our world as we know, has passed through so much of sorrow, so much of pain, so much of anxiety, that sometimes people dream that the pain of our creation outweighs its joy. Their larger knowledge made the appearance of our world a matter for rejoicing through the spheres, and those Sons of God of the Hebrew are spoken of in Indian scriptures as the mighty Builders of worlds. And they tell us that whenever there is a new emanation of a system, that then the creative WORD, whom they call BRAHMÂ, brings with Him the fruitage of a previous universe; those who in a previous universe have grown into superhuman perfection, they tell us, are gathered up into the Life of the Great Builder, and carried on with Him to His next creative task. And They are the first who are embodied forth, They the first who are sent out into partially separated life, and They are the results of the past made perfect to a certain limit of perfection, the thought of the LOGOS of that time; and They come to help.

Now the word "Building" will be familiar to many of you, for what is a well-known term used by Masons as regards the Supreme? They call Him the Great Architect of the Universe. But what do they mean by that famous phrase? They use it constantly, and speak of it as a fact they recognise and know. But what does the "Architect" mean? Where is an architect worthy of the name who does not plan before he begins the building? The architect is the maker of the plan, and what right have men to use that term at all of the Supreme unless they recognise that the wisdom of past ages gave a proper title to the Supreme Emanator of Worlds? These words ought not to be mere empty phrases in the mouths of any of you. Why should you use a term like that and mean nothing by it, and think nothing about it? And why should those who worship the Great Architect of the Universe call themselves Masons at all, unless they in their measure are also builders in varied grades of knowledge and of power? For those ancient things that have come down to us out of the past and that are worked in ceremonies and symbols, every great name in them has a meaning; every great ceremony indicates a process in Nature; and what use for us to take the ancient drapings unless we have within the garments those mighty verities hidden from the minds of the thoughtless and the ignorant, hidden from the outer world but known to the student of the Mysteries? And it might be well, perchance, if some of you would think over it from the inner standpoint, and see whether you, at least, who call on the name of the Great Architect may not learn something of His Plan for our world—for that is big enough for us.

Thinking then on that, what would naturally come after the Great Architect Himself? Those Sons of God who are to build the new universe, the new world. And then we begin looking at the many Scriptures again, passing from one source of thought to another, as we gain something from each. And we learn from the Christian book of the *Revelation* that ever around the throne of the LOGOS there are Those who are called the Seven Spirits. And those are recognised by all the great religions; go back as far as you will to the most ancient faith you can study, and you will find there are ever seven of those subsidiary great Builders, each with his own share of the Plan made by the Architect for His whole system.

And so, as you go on, you begin to realise that there are great grades of superhuman Beings, and that They all co-operate in the working out of the Plan, and according to Their grade, Their work, and according to Their powers, Their duty, and Their responsibility. You can get the sketch of your building and see how you go from the Architect to His chief Overseers, and then to Those who look after smaller portions of the work; and you know that you may go down and down until you come not only to the bricklayers who lay on the foundation traced in the part of the Architect's Plan which is their special work, but even to the labourers who bring the bricks and the labourers who mix the mortar that may be wanted, and the workmen who cut and carve the stones. And very often the stones may seem incongruous and without a place to fit in, and yet they are ever wanted when the Plan has reached the point at which the stone which seemed to be unfit becomes necessary for the completion of a portion of the work.

And so the sentence is thrown out, significant in its meaning, that the stone which the builders rejected has become the headstone of the corner. And so as you go along you realise that it is likely in a system so orderly as ours, in a system which is a realm of law, that there *is* such a Plan, very likely some Plan, which, if we could discover, then with it we might co-operate. That we need not perhaps remain blind workers who know nothing of the Plan on which we are employed, but open-eyed workers who have caught glimpses perhaps of their part at least in the Plan, and so can work with a bright intelligence, and bring their own thought as well as hands to the perfecting of the fragment of the Plan which their Overseer has in hand. And then there dawns upon us along this line of thought that where the Plan is so mighty as the one for our system, the fragment that belongs to our world must be comparatively small—and because smaller more within the grasp of our thought, more within the reach of our very limited capacities. And then we begin to try to search in history for traces of the Plan, for connected happenings, for similar events. And out of that complexity of happenings there begins to shine, as it were underneath, certain lines, and as we follow them, these lines we see are portions of a Plan; much that is incomprehensible, because only a portion, much that may not have its perfected purpose here; but in the joining with other portions it is vital that every part should be true to the Plan, that every part should be carried through so that each portion of the Plan is perfect, and, so far as completeness for a fragment is possible, may show a certain perfection, a limited perfection in itself. And then we begin to search and ponder and think, and we catch a gleam of at least one purpose which is behind our world. Looking around us we see various kingdoms, as we call them, of Nature—the mineral, the vegetable, the animal, and the human, and some stop there, and some go on to the superhuman—not supernatural, but superhuman.

We can realise it as a rational, reasonable thing that the will of a part shall be in consonance with the will of the whole; that a smaller self shall adapt himself to the helping and perfecting of the larger Self; and that it is a very probable purpose of this universe to produce human beings who shall voluntarily choose the best, voluntarily associate themselves with the Law, voluntarily not only recognise the Supreme Will, but strive to become a part of it, identical with it, and carrying it out within their limited measure. And we say at length: What is a man? And looking over those kingdoms I have just spoken of, we find that we may define a man by his relation to the greater law. For, thinking of the mineral, the vegetable, the animal, we see that law is imposed on them by a superior will. They have not yet evolved to will, they are moved by desire; and the difference between desire and will, the difference in us between desire and will, is that desire arises by promptings of want from within, cravings of the material nature for sustenance, answered by objects from without, the objects of desire surrounding us on every side to draw out desires, and that those desires are determined by the result of the impact, whether it causes pleasure or causes pain. Where it causes pleasure we desire the impact to be repeated, and where it causes pain we seek to avoid another impact of a similar nature. As long as a man's actions are determined by the promptings of desire, so long he has not yet evolved the mighty power of Will. For Will is that divine quality which is Self-determined—not determined by attractions or repulsions which play upon the outer nature. Now in the animal desire rules. He seeks what his nature craves for, and he shrinks from that which gives him pain, and he is obedient to the law of his nature. He does not rebel; he does not resist; he follows the law as imposed upon him, unknowingly, unconsciously; thus the law works for his evolution. He struggles with other animals; he fights for his own life; he destroys where a life seems to increase his own; he is moved continually by the satisfying of his cravings, and unconsciously by that he evolves. It is true, as has often been pointed out, and as Huxley quoted from the East: "The law of the survival of the fittest is the law of evolution for the brute." That law he follows, and he knows no better. Why should he? The law impels him—compels him; and by obedience to that he evolves.

Then we pass on into what we call the human kingdom. And looking at that human kingdom we find some qualities we call animal qualities and some that we recognise as of a higher scale, and we call them human. And man disobeys the law; he resists the law; is a rebel against the law. He desires that which serves him, that gives him pleasure. He grasps at all he wants, careless at first what may be the effect upon others; and when he finds he cannot always have what he wants, he is angry and discontented. The beginning of Man lies in his rebellion against law. That is the first step. He is understanding a little more of himself, and he realises that he is able to disobey the law. He does not realise that the law itself is inviolable, and breaks those who disobey in the long run. He thinks he can get along pleasing himself, satisfying himself, grasping everything and disregarding every-one around him; and still he seems to follow a law of struggle, and does follow it like the law of the beasts of the jungle. Nay! he has not even yet quite left that stage nor realised that in obedience to law will lie his ultimate happiness. But gradually and slowly he does learn a law other than the law to which the brute pays; compelled obedience. He learns there is something higher than grasping. That a keener pleasure sometimes comes from sacrificing than from seizing. Love is the great teacher. Love is the great educator. Love the great evolver. And the man gradually learns that a personal sacrifice for something, for another whom he loves, gives a greater satisfaction to his human nature than a grasping at that by which a beloved one suffers. And then he begins dimly to grope after some other law, and he learns that the great law of human love is not the law of the survival of the fittest, but the law of the sacrifice of the stronger to the weaker, of the greater to the lesser, in order that the lesser may also share in his own life. And by very very slow degrees he begins to see he is only a part of a larger whole, and that he is as the cell in a body, and that the cell should subserve the purpose of the whole body, first of the organ to which it belongs, and then in the organ, the service, the happiness of the body as a whole. And with that there comes to him a great light. He begins to see that the part should work for the whole and not only for the part which is its lower self. That it is a greater and more noble and more human thing to sacrifice individual inclinations and individual gains and to work with the Power that makes for Righteousness. And he begins to see in the world the working of that Power in its successes, in the things it breaks as well as in the things it supports; and deliberately, of set volition of his own, that Will awakens in him—that Will which is his higher quality—not the will merely to live, but the will to live for others and to help in the building of a happier and a better world. And when evolution has gone so far in this evolving man, in whom divinity is un-folding more and more rapidly, there conies the time when his will is no longer separate; when his will realises itself as part of the divine Will which is evolving the worlds to higher, to grander levels. And willingly, joyfully, he associates himself with that Will, until he can say: "Lo, I live to do Thy Will, O God!" When he is thus Self-determined, when by long experience, by bitter pain, he has learnt that true happiness lies in harmonising the lower will with the higher, and when that has become harmonised in him so that it cannot change, then he passes out of the human into the superhuman realms of being—but not before. And it is those who have reached that stage in evolution, those whose will is perfectly harmonised with the divine, those who live to obey the law of life and to serve their brothers—those are They who form the Inner Government of the World, the Power that makes for Righteousness. There, behind all that we call "powers" in this world, are the superhuman Rulers, the superhuman Teachers, the superhuman Powers—intellectual, mental, emotional, passional, material—that play their part in the building up of the world. Those are at the back of all the great religions. Those are at the back of all the great civilisations. Those are They whom all nations have recognised. They are sometimes called, as in India, Rishis; sometimes they are called Sages; sometimes Prophets of the highest range. And They are ever at work to bring human wills into consonance with the divine by helping them, by inspiring them, by holding before them mighty ideals. They are the true Rulers and the true Teachers; They the real Powers that guide our world in evolution. And because that is so you cannot separate religion and morality from the outer things of life. Religion is everything or it is nothing. Morality is the one foundation, or nothing can endure. Is it to be said that morals have no place in politics? that morals have no place amongst statesmen? that morals have no place amongst the rulers, of the temporary masters, of the world? Not so did they think in ancient days, in those older days when humanity was more easily shaped and guided because more childlike in their looking up as the child looks up to his parents, to the great superhuman Rulers of the world. In those days it was the duty of such men to visit the court of every King, and see whether he was ruling according to righteousness and guiding and helping and guarding his people. Turn to some of the old stories and read of the visits of Those, the great Inner Governors of the World, to the outer governors whom they put to shape and guide those older Nations. You will find the most political and social questions addressed to the King. "Do you see that your artificers are supplied with the materials of their crafts?" That is one of the questions you might read. "Do you support the widows and orphans of those soldiers who have perished in fighting your battles?" "Do you see that your agriculturalists are well supplied with seed, and with all the necessaries for the feeding of your people?" These were the sort of questions that were asked of the Kings in those days by Those whom they recognised as their spiritual superiors. Are we then to be told in these later days that it is not the business of those who, however imperfectly, try to uphold religious and moral ideals before the Nations: "It is no business of yours to interfere with governments and social arrangements; leave these alone"? What is the business of the religious man, if it be not the guiding of the Nation in the path of righteousness, and the rebuking of wrong wherever that wrong is, and however highly placed it may be? If they fail in that duty, of what use is their religion to the Nation? If they shrink from that responsibility, what right have they to talk of other worlds when they do not try to improve the world in which they are living at the time? They of all others ought to be able to point out the path of righteousness, because they are less immediately concerned with all the confusing problems of the outer life of to-day, because they should be men of prayer and meditation, studying the deeper thoughts that underlie the workings of the Supreme. Just because their eyes should be wider open and less clouded by personal desires and personal prejudices, therefore they must help to guide the Nation—not in the details of its political struggles, but in the great religious and moral laws without which a Nation must perish—by the Great Law of Brotherhood. And so it is for them above all others to study the divine Plan, to mark where Nations are going wrong, before they have gone so far wrong as to be almost beyond human mending. You see how this will lead us into considering the principles on which we are to try to rebuild our shattered civilisation. To do without religion is to do without the Light which lights our path. To say that morality is a matter for individuals and not a matter for Nations is to betray the great principles of obedience to that moral law which is the safeguard of national and international life.

And if any of you can realise that there is a possibility of the kind of Plan that 1 have been suggesting; that we may find out what that Plan is, and guide our lives thereby; that we may by study, by thought, by meditation, by self-sacrifice, clear our eyes enough to have the vision of a Plan for human life and human evolution; if you have caught one glimpse of that at any time,—then you will realise there is nothing else worth living for in life save to co-operate with that Plan and hasten the happiness of man. You will realise that it is worth while to live, whether your life be joyous or sorrowful, if you can co-operate in making the world a little better, a little less sad for the great masses of its population. You will realise that the object of human life is to bring the will of the individual into accord with the will of the Highest ; and having brought that will into accord, then to work to carry it out among men; for knowledge that bears no fruit in action is useless to humanity; knowledge worked out for human helping, forwards the salvation of the world.

Lecture II
The Outer Methods The World's Opportunity

FRIENDS: I took as a title for this evening's talk the words "The Outer Methods—The World's Opportunity". And I want to try to show you this evening how that mighty Life, which we were trying to look at last week, shows itself in manifestation in our world; how it unfolds its power and its beauty; how forms are builded; how the real method might be put in one word, the word "Evolution," if science had made that—as it seems inclined to do now—if it had made that a double process, the Life involving itself in matter and then unfolding itself in the infinite multitude of forms, becoming more and more complex as the world grows older, passing from one stage to another in ever greater unfoldment of the infinite possibilities of the Life. I am going to take evolution in that double way, for science leaves us somewhat puzzled as regards the impulse which causes the wonderful evolution of forms—speaks vaguely of a force that draws from the front and of a force that presses from behind; but those are rather words perhaps than a very definite thinking and grasping of the reasons and the methods of the unfolding. Life, I put to you, is at the very heart, whether of our world or of the universe. Life, a manifestation of that mighty Life in which is all, Past, Present, and Future, of which I spoke last week.

When we begin to deal with our own world we are then in a region where we can trace the details of such evolution; where we can try and grasp the intimate method of the unfoldment. And so we may gradually learn to understand the workings of our own consciousness, finding them to be the reflections of the mightier Consciousness that creates and upholds and regenerates the worlds. And looking at it for a moment from this standpoint of the Life, we try to see everywhere Life showing out its capacities and shaping matter, as we call it, for the expression of those capacities. We realise that Life is one, however multiple its manifestations. Just as we might regard electricity as one force in Nature, though showing itself in different ways as heat, as light, and so on, according to the nature or resistance of the matter through which it is manifesting itself.

That unity of Life—dealing with it only as it is shown in the many living things of our own earth—has been, as you know, demonstrated comparatively recently by that great Indian scientist, Sir Jagadish Chandra Bose, who had been experimenting over long, long years on mineral and vegetable, striving to search out if it were true that the Life in them was the Life in the animal and in the human, only more narrowly conditioned in its manifestations. For many years he strove to prove it, to prove it in a scientific way against much of prejudice, against age-long ideas which divided Nature into the living and the non-living, whereas his contention was that there was no such thing as a non-living nature, but that all Nature was the expression of a Life. And lately he succeeded in demonstrating to the world of science here the truth of his contention, which he said was based on an ancient sentence in the language of his own land, the Samskrit, a verse that he said was sung by his ancestors on the banks of the river Gaṅgā, and he was only showing by scientific demonstration the great truth so long before spoken by a divinely illuminated Teacher. And he showed by his experiments how Life responded, whether you took it in the vegetable or the animal. How it was similarly affected by drugs, by intoxicants and soporifics of various sorts, and how the response of the indwelling Life could be traced and shown in similar results, different as was the form in which that Life was manifesting. That great demonstration is full of interest to those of us who had taken from the great scriptures of the world, from the teachings of all religions, that Life really lay behind all manifestations of material things, and came forth from the ONE LIFE, the Limitless, the Incomprehensible, from which come forth stream after stream, manifesting itself in what we call matter.

Then, looking for a moment at the many religions of the world, we find an expression used in most of them—and in all of them so far as the qualities shown are recognised and seen—that Life in the universe creates; that Life bodies itself in forms which it sustains and upholds; that Life, when the form no longer will yield to its impulse, breaks it and casts it aside, and regenerates for itself another form fitted for a further progress of the indwelling Life. So that in thinking of the Life as one, we recognise that it shows itself out in the worlds in this triple form which religion has often called a Trinity, which shows really aspects of the Life, manifestations of the Life, Life remaining ever ONE and showing itself out in this threefold fashion.

Then we take a step further, and we realise that in our human consciousness the same unity, the same triplicity, may be seen. For as we think of ourselves we feel our unity, we feel that we are one, that our consciousness is one, that it is our very Self, that which is deepest within us, most real in us, that which impels us to action, to feeling, to thought. And we see that we also have one Self, or rather are one Self, who shows himself as Life, or Consciousness, in a similar triple fashion. For, looking at human consciousness in the ordinary way, we see in that that consciousness shows itself as Will, as Wisdom, as Awareness of an outer world, and that these three, as we shall see in a moment, are conditioned by the nature of the matter in which the Life is shown forth, each great aspect of the Life appropriating to itself a special kind of matter, the vibrations in the matter responding to the changes in the moods in consciousness. Seeing ourselves thus, as a unity, manifesting as a triplicity, we then begin to examine somewhat into the matter in which this Life is endeavouring to express himself. And we find that in our physical world, when we study ourselves, we can recognise certain higher and lower manifestations. We realise, if we take the Awareness, that we have the synthetic in the Intellect that combines that we have, in what we sometimes call the Mind, the lower manifestation, that which analyses; and that those two main qualities may be said to differentiate within Awareness; Intellect as the higher power of thought in man, and the concrete, reasoning Mind as its manifestation in a denser form of matter. And so we also realise that we have duality in our world again—Wisdom in the higher manifesting as Love in the lower, the great power which holds all together, while the mind separates by analysis, and then, out of those separated factors, the intellect builds up some great idea and synthesises them into one. And so we find also that Will, showing itself in the lower world as desire, motives all Activity. And in those three of Mind and Love—that we may call emotion—and Activity, the consciousness that we feel down here in our waking world manifests itself, in these three ways, neither less nor more. In that practically all psychology, eastern and western, is agreed, with slight differences of terms but with a unity of thought. And the difference of terms that we find in the East is very largely because their psychology is a very ancient science, while in the West it is comparatively modern. So that in the East it has been worked out very much into detail, into a very complicated science, whereas in the West it is only growing somewhat into that complexity, but has not yet existed long enough over here to make the same intricate researches that have been made in the older countries of the world.

Glancing over that rough sketch, and trying, as it were, to put it into a form which will enable us to trace out our methods in involution and evolution, we realise that science, western science, helps us enormously in the details of evolution; has gathered together such a mass of observations, has classified them with such care, has marked out their resemblances and their differences so clearly, that it gives us an enormous mass of knowledge, gained by the study of phenomena in this our own physical world, which enables us to understand very much better the larger generalisations which we sometimes find in religions—those greater, wider outlines which are given to us by men who have climbed through all stages of humanity until they have passed beyond the cycle of life and death, constantly alternating, and have reached a perfection of human organisation, a perfection of body, of emotion, of mind, which has enabled them to climb into the higher worlds where the origins of these lower manifestations are to be found, and so to reach a greater unity behind the manifold differences in the lower world. And to some extent science is recognising involution in these modern days, although not exactly as the ancients put it; but the root-thought is the same. If you knew the immense change that came over science—I was going to say since our own time, but I am almost afraid to say that now that I am so old, and am speaking to so many whose time-measures are of a shorter space; when I was young, I may say, science was then looking on matter as the chief thing. You will remember that famous phrase of Tyndall's, that everyone knows although it has become antiquated, that we must look to matter for the promise and the potency of every form of life. That was the thought in my younger days in the scientific world, and that there were many organs in different bodies, and that these practically created their functions; it was not until very much later—more, I think, than twenty years afterwards—that that dictum of Tyndall was turned quite upside down by Sir William Crookes, when occupying the same chair in the British Association for the Advancement of Science, and he exactly reversed it, and said that we must see in Life the creator and moulder of matter. And that is the view that has since swept everything before it, because further experiment and further observation and more careful and accurate analysis have shown that in the very simplest form of living matter—and all matter lives —the whole fragment—we can call it nothing else—performs every function which is necessary for the sustenance of life, and that by the very performance of those functions of life continuously the surrounding matter is shaped into organs which limit the part of that fragment which performs a particular function. And the life and the function continually going on, working and working, and repeating itself and repeating itself as the life is maintained, forms more and more perfect organs for its own varied functions; so that, instead of the old view that the organ in some wonderful way gives rise to the function, we have the far simpler idea that may be observed in Nature—that it is the function that shapes the organ. And some of you, looking back, may remember the very graphic way in which William Kingdon Clifford tried to explain that to the children. When he wanted to get the children to understand a little what evolution meant, he put it in a very simple and graphic way, and he told them about that great kingdom in Nature out of which the birds and the reptiles, as we know them later, arose. He said that some of these indeterminate creatures desired to crawl, and they became reptiles; and others tried to fly, and they became birds. That is, that the will to exercise a function determines the line of evolution of the creature; and although it was put as a story, an explanation for children, it contains one of the profoundest truths of Nature: that it is the Will, the will to live, the will to think, the will to see, the will to hear, that forms the organs whereby all those functions, that are willed by the Life itself, shape matter into organs that enable that Life to express itself more completely, more perfectly, to unfold more and more of that particular capacity by means of the organ it created in a simpler form. Thus there is this constant interaction of Life and Form; the Life willing and the Form adapting itself, the Life thinking—I have no other word I can use—and thus creating, the Life supporting and continuing and finally breaking the outworn form. And so we have this picture of an ever-changing world in which the bodies and in which the Life have become more and more complex, and the Life unfolds itself in ever larger and larger capacities; and so the whole great world of living things is built up: in the mineral world we see attraction and repulsion, affinities and disintegrations; and in the vegetable world we see those moods showing themselves out more fully as sensations; and in the animal world more perfectly still, showing out as desires and cravings; and in the world of man yet more fully, by the working of the mind, reflection of intellect, and so showing out completely that great triplicity of life.

When from that we turn to ask a little as to how this Life involves itself and whether any stages of involution can be seen, we come across a very remarkable succession which is pictured for us in this world—which is really a reflection of the higher world of thought—which is pictured for us in the way that the Life involves itself into form in the embryo which is to become the human being. We see it elsewhere in all forms of life, tracing it from its new conception to its outward manifestation, as a particular kind of plant, of animal, of human, embryo; and those pictures in the lower world are not to be despised, for they sometimes help us to understand a little more clearly, and to glimpse a little more fully, the marvellous way in which in the higher, subtler worlds the Life bodies itself forth. For, when the ONE that we speak of as the LOGOS or the WORD—as I said to you last Sunday, the manifestation of this great Life in its divine aspect—when the Logos begins a new universe, we read hints and suggestions in ancient, very ancient, books that to some extent—a very limited extent—are verifiable by those who will take the trouble and give the time to evolve in themselves some of the higher powers of the Life a little in advance of the ordinary evolution of man ; for you must remember that human thought and human intelligence applied to the expansion of consciousness may expand consciousness very much more rapidly than Nature itself, if left unassisted by the human mind in the long, long climbing upwards, the evolution of humanity can do, and that just as in the lower worlds you may evolve a type more rapidly by neutralising laws that oppose you and utilising laws that help you, whether in the plant or in the animal kingdom—it is constantly done—so may man, if he realises the laws of mind, if he understands something of the world of consciousness and the expansion thereof, so may he quicken that expansion of consciousness and be able to reach higher worlds than our physical, differentiated from us by the greater subtlety of their matter, but all of them material, however fine and subtle that material of them may be. Taking advantage of that, there are phrases we may find in some of the ancient books which we are apt to take as purely metaphysical, allegorical, and pictorial, call it what you will; and we find, for instance, in a great Indian book put into the mouth of God the words: "I am the Life-Breath." The thought would be more familiar to you if I quoted them from the Hebrew scripture, where it is written: "By the word of the Lord were the heavens made; and all the host of them by the breath of his mouth" (Psalm xxxiii. 6).

Now Breath is sometimes said to be Life and Life to be Breath, and in those lofty regions the word Breath is not an ill-chosen word to use for the great outbreathing of the divine Life which, gathering together from the boundless realms of space a certain quantity of that far, far-off matter, makes, as it were, a ring round it, in which He is going to build up His new system, and breathes His life into that enclosed root-matter, as it is sometimes called; and by that Breath—if I may take a very common illustration from right down here in the physical world, as you may, if you breathe into a glass of water, create little vacua which are not really vacua, but are filled with your breath and shelled with a little film of water—creates the matter out of which He will build His special system, His worlds. In that form, subtle beyond our thinking, minute beyond our imagination—and yet if for a moment you will think of that building of a single form to which I just now alluded—you will know that from a single cell you get a whole group of cells by the forming within that simple cell of little lines of division, not separating them off into separate things but making a mass of conjoined, adherent cells, so bodying forth for us under our eyes, as it were, the great picture of creative activity—first Unity, the One, then within that Unity the delicate lines of separation, making the many, still in union, these marked-out parts of future difference being still joined together; and then, later, in some forms of living creatures you may see the breaking asunder of these subdivided cells, and there you come to the picture of the great separative principle, the intellect, at work, with its offspring of the mind. And then still further, passing downwards ever, you come to the appearance, in still denser form of matter, of what we call attraction and repulsion, of what we call love and hate when we come to human beings. And when you examine those you begin to realise that the Life, which is one, is ever seeking to reunite itself with the several portions of itself that the impulse has divided coming down, but that the Life in each separated form seeks the Life in other separated forms and tries to draw them together, and the forms resist it, and the incongruous forms repulse it, and a constant struggle goes on between the Life which is seeking reunion and the forms which are insisting on their separateness ; and you see how the forms gather in fresh material in order that by grasping they may grow, and how the Life is ever seeking to give itself out to find union with other lives, until we find ourselves down here in a physical world of matter, and see its constant struggle, its constant opposition between the indwelling Life desiring to unite and the forms resisting, for fear that in the union they should lose their individuality and no longer know themselves as living beings.

Now I have spoken of different worlds here. I mean by that, different types of matter. It is not difficult for you to realise that; if you think of our physical world only, you have solid, you have liquid, you have gas and you have ether, but you may have those all in one type of matter. You may have physical matter, which shows itself as solid in the ice, as liquid in the water, as vapour in the steam; and above that they tell us there are ethers in which all the great forces play, which affect the denser matter, but are not themselves directly cognisable yet by human skill, being intangible. And knowing that that is so in our physical world, it is not difficult to realise, I think, that you may have different types of matter analogous to those. That, speaking comparatively, you might think of your physical world as representing the more solid forms of matter, the denser forms, I call them; and then you might think of another type of matter above them, where the matter was far less dense, which answers specially to those moods of consciousness that we call the emotions and the passions and the feelings. And then you might have yet a third type of matter—I am ascending at the moment—in which the moods of consciousness we call thought embody themselves, so that with every change of thought there is in that mental world a form bodied forth, which is the thought-form, as we call it, seen by a large number of people to-day, and by an ever-increasing number. And that, coming up beyond that mental and intellectual world, you would then be coming—after the great division of the intellect—you would then be coming into union once again, corresponding to the union in the descending life, and beyond that yet we may dream of unity, where the Oneness is recognised by all.

I would ask you, if you can, for a moment to keep that ladder in your mind. The descending Life, which at first is One, coming from the divine world where separation is not; and this great wave of Life comes down as a unity, the Spirit in man. And next, it comes into a world of slightly denser matter, and then union is the predominant mark; and next it comes into a world of yet denser matter, and then separation becomes the dominant note in that world. And still further down it comes into yet denser matter, where forms are denser, showing itself forth as feeling that strives to unite, and the form that tries to keep separate; until finally you arrive at your physical world, where these last three types are manifest as our human consciousness, as body, emotion, and thought.

Suppose now that Life turns upward again and begins to climb. It will have to climb, enriched with all its long experiences, fuller, more complex, far more wonderful; and carrying these with it upwards in its climb, it will pass out of the great separation of dense matter here—which is ever being consumed in the using—and pass upward into the world of the emotions, where love and hate are struggling, attraction and repulsion; and then into the world of the intellect, where there will be still separation, and strong individuality showing itself in human beings. And when you have reached that point, where we now are, then you may begin to forecast what the next great advance of humanity will be—that it must be towards union. That is the next upward rung, as it were, the second downward rung in the involution of the Life, and that as the Life in descending took to itself an atom of every one of these worlds of our fivefold universe, and gathered round itself more of the matter of that world to form a sheath or body for the expression of itself, so, after that downward descent was completed and the activity of the Life was turned upwards, it would after a certain time reach that same world of union through which it passed in its long descent into grosser, and grosser, and grosser matter. And when we begin to enquire a little more closely as to how it is that all this great, this tremendous accumulation of powers, of capacities, which the Life gathers round itself is achieved, what is the method by which that gathering is made and individualised, then you come to that central idea of the great religions, the idea of the Reincarnation of the human Spirit. The Spirit is ever leaving the material bodies in which he clothes himself and which, being material, are subject to decay. "God created man to be immortal," it is said in one of the Hebrew Scriptures, called apocryphal by the Christian Church, "and made him in the image of His own Eternity". Every man in the image of God is eternal as God Himself is eternal, and that is the pledge of Life on the other side of death, although it goes far, far, far beyond that. Man is eternal in his nature, and can only be subject to death so far as his outer casing is concerned. HE cannot die. The gathering of faculties is, as I said, by reincarnation. Now think for a moment over what that means, for I have not time to go into details. There are three of these outer coatings of the Eternal Spirit in man in the three worlds of mind, of feeling, and of action respectively. These are the three worlds in which he evolves his forms and unfolds his powers. Living here in the physical world he is clothed in a triple body: the body through which he expresses activity; this one that you see, our dense body; permeating this is the finer body in which he expresses emotions; and, permeating both, is the still finer body in which he expresses thought. But, being material, they are all perishable. They are not made in the image of God's Eternity. And so, it being a peculiarity of matter that it is resistant, that it cannot without disintegration be pressed beyond a certain point, that in building up a form that form is able to grow, taking from the particular world to which it belongs more and more matter, assimilating it, transmuting it into its own special kind of material, and so going on growing and growing. But the physical body reaches the limit of its growth. Emotions in their own body go on while the physical body is decaying. Thought in its own body goes on while the physical body is disintegrating. They are reflections of those greater spiritual originals of which I spoke, of Intellect, of Wisdom, and of Will, that cannot perish. But these bodies of matter, each of which in turn disintegrates—what should the embodied Spirit do when these bodies reach the limit of their growth, when they reach the limit of their flexibility, when they reach the limit of their adaptation to their several environments, and begin to lessen in vigour, to decay in parts, and to threaten total dissolution? What can he do save seek another set of forms, inasmuch as he has not unfolded the wonderful wealth of his life? And that is what reincarnation means; he passes through these three worlds of action, of emotion, and of thought. The religions call them by many names. They speak of the physical world as the mortal world; then they speak of an intermediate world, which is not more closely or precisely described; and then they speak of a heavenly world. I am using the words which express accurately the type of the matter of which these three worlds are made: our dense matter which is used for action, the rather finer matter which is used for emotion, and the yet finer which is made for thought. Now how do these conduce—for the duration of these three makes a life cycle, a life period—how do they conduce to the gathering of experience and the enriching of the human being in the next birth? In the world of action he sets many causes going by his relationships with his fellow-men. He causes happiness, he causes misery. He follows vices or he follows virtues. In the early stages he does not know the difference between right and wrong. He does not know that laws are around him, and that if he strikes himself against a law he has to suffer. That is a thing he has yet to learn in these bodies which his life informs, and in this world it is that he gathers the material for this knowledge gradually by experience. But he cannot gather all the experience he wants, because a life is too short a time for all the causes he sets going to work out. He may kill a man, if he is a savage, and that man goes out of his way, and the surrounding morality of the tribe does not blame him if the man is not of his tribe, but a man of some other tribe, because at first their views of morality are very limited. He has yet to learn that killing is against the law of Nature for man, it comes within the scope of the moral law; and he learns that on the other side of death in the region of the emotions. I am putting this to you briefly and asserting it, but you can read all about it, if you feel inclined. In that intermediate world he reaps the result of the—not violations of law, which are impossible, but of the—actions that disregard the law, whether he knows it or not. You may say: Is that just? Is it just that when a child puts his hand into the fire, not knowing that the fire burns, he suffers? The answer is: It is the condition of the future knowledge of the child; he can never know, unless he comes up against laws, that he cannot break them; and as he cannot break them he bruises himself, and so he gathers knowledge. By that he gathers knowledge of Nature on the one side by suffering, and he gathers knowledge on the other side when he is in accord with the law; and in accord with the law he finds happiness. As the Lord Buddha once said, speaking to an ignorant crowd: "Sorrow follows on wrongdoing, as the wheels of the cart follow the heels of the ox. Happiness follows on right doing, as the wheels of the cart follow the heels of the ox." He put it in a way that the peasants round him could appreciate—the inviolability of moral as of physical law. In that intermediate stage the man learns his lessons, some of them, and takes a long time in the learning; and then that emotional body breaks away from him, and he goes into what is called the heavenly world, that we call the mental world, in his mind body, and there the thoughts that he has had during his physical life here, they are the food on which the Spirit feeds.[1] It is a world where the hard and cruel things are kept outside, walled in, as it were, for the teaching of that side of the life of this disembodied Spirit, and all that he has thought nobly works itself out into mental faculty; and all that he has thought of service works itself out into greater capacity for service; and all that he has thought of art works itself out into greater capacity for beauty; and all that he has studied into greater capacity of mind; for the heaven world is the world of the growth and the flowering of all the seeds that we have sown in the sheath of our mortal body, that we call the mental body—our germs of thought there grow, grow into flower, grow into fruit; that is, they change into faculties, and these are brought back as the mental faculties, the mental capacity, when the Spirit embodies himself again in a new body which is shaped for the expression of the thoughts and the emotions that he brings back, and you call these "character" and "temperament". Children are born with very different characters, because they have led very different lives, and different numbers of lives in the past. That is why there are no favourites in Nature; God is absolute Justice. The child born with a noble character has won that

---

[1] It must be remembered that the triple Spirit is clothed throughout the human life from individualisation to initiation in a permanent though evolving body, the causal body, with the sheaths of his two other aspects; and that the permanent atoms of the mental, emotional, and physical bodies, with all the new possibilities latent within them, are stored up in the causal body, and are sent forth from it as the nuclei of the next mortal bodies, when the Spirit reincarnates.

character by ages of struggle, by ages of toil, by many and many a defeat, and many and many a victory, until at last he has shaped that character and brings it back again to earth to serve the world. That is the great hope of reincarnation, why it is a true gospel for men, universal in the old religions and spreading rapidly today. For men feel that the immense inequalities of human capacity, of human power, of human mind, and of human physical strength and health, that these are so desperately different in the babes that are born into the world, that some never have a chance while others can hardly fail to be successful; one is born a genius or a saint, and the other is born an idiot or a criminal; and these frightful inequalities in nature would be heart-breaking did we not know that it is a difference of age, that is, a difference in the period at which a particular Spirit entered into this world of evolution, and one has had very little time in which to unfold himself, and is still in the grip of this intractable matter, that is, the matter of our physical world, and the other has had a long time and has largely mastered it. And the cravings, and the longings, and the desires of the old experiences are behind the latter, and whisper to him whether he shall yield or resist; and as out of long experience he has learnt that to go against the law brings misery, and to go with the law means happiness, therefore it is that the accumulated experience, laid up in that great reservoir of the Spirit within him, what you call conscience, is found in the older and therefore the more developed children when they are born into the world. And if you say to such a child, "It is wrong to hurt another," the child responds at once; that which is within him of his own experience, that realises that you are telling him the truth. And if you say the same thing to a savage child, there is no response; he has not yet gathered the experience that we speak of as conscience. And that, very roughly, is the way in which reincarnation works. It is a particular phase of evolution applied in this particular way to human beings. There are other forms of it in the lower kingdoms; I am dealing here with man.

Now what applies to one man applies also to Nations and to Races. That which you can trace of order in the individual, you can also, if you will study, trace as of order in the civilisations and the development of the Races in our world. You will see at once that that is a very, very long subject, and when I say a Race I mean by that, in the fullest sense of the word, what we call a Root-Race, a Mother-Race. But in speaking thus I mean by that the kind of differences you see in outer form and appearance and everything, between say an ordinary Negro, a Chinese or Japanese, and an Aryan. I take these three successive types of the third, fourth, and fifth Root-Races to show you what I mean by a Root-Race; that is, a Race that has a common likeness in all its branches by which you can distinguish it from other Root-Races, although the mingling of them may blur the likeness to some extent; you will have a certain form of head and a certain setting and cutting of the features. And if for a moment you will take the Aryan Race from its cradle in Central Asia, you will find there the root of that marked difference from the Mongolians and other Asian Nations that surrounded its cradle; and then you will find certain emigrations going out from it and populating the Western World. Think of that Root-Race as one which contains in it the germs of faculties and powers and emotions, the physical peculiarities which are to be developed one after another in these emigrations which I speak of, which left the cradle-land and went off westwards. Now these branches of the Root-Race differ very much less from each other and have a common likeness of type. They differ in colour very often; they differ in qualities very much. You cannot develop by evolution at the same time qualities that are antagonistic one to the other. You have to separate dominant qualities, and then to develop, generally to excess, in a sub-type, or sub-race, and later on to prune away the excess and bring about a reunion. For evolution is like a great sea in which there are successive waves. You know the rising tide does not run straight ahead all the time. It goes on in waves, and a wave forms, rises, breaks, and runs backward again; and so do these Races and sub-races of man; they are like the waves in a coming tide, and as the tide rises the waves break and retreat, but the tide made of successive waves advances; for a while one wave is in front of another; and so in the evolution of a great Race, you have this Root-Stock, or Mother-Race, that I spoke of, in which you find enormous variety, the germs which are going to be developed separately, the great distinctive qualities which will be developed separately in the sub-races, and these will have marked characteristics. There will be something that will dominate a sub-race amid all the many human qualities which it will evolve, which colours as it were the whole of them and marks them as belonging to a particular type, or sub-division, of man.

Now if you look at the Root-Stock, it is of course the remainder of the Āryans who, after the emigrations, went south-wards into India, those who are now called the Indo-Aryans, to distinguish them from the emigrants who went westwards—four sets of them.

You have that which went into Egypt, the first emigration, or second sub-race, and they developed particularly the physical body, in its inner mechanism and its relations to the other and subtler worlds, what was called "the Wisdom of Egypt," or the recognition of the relationships between the surrounding subtler worlds and the physical man in the physical worlds. Its "wise men" worked from the physical body, and a very deep knowledge of that—not only of what you can see of the physical body, but also of the subtler, or etheric, parts of it. And its Science is marked by the peculiarity that it began always with the science that you reject as science, thinking that your modern physical presentment is the whole of Science, forgetting that Science should "weave for God the garment thou seest Him by". That is to say, they began with Astrology and worked on to Astronomy, they began with Alchemy and worked on to Chemistry, and so on. And this was the great characteristic of that emigration which went to Egypt, and which spread southwards in Africa, and also went along the borders of the Mediterranean.

Then you get the next, the second emigration or third sub-race, which goes to Persia. And there you had the peculiar note, the note of Purity, which dealt not only with thought and emotion, but also with the elements, as the Ancients called them, the Earth, the Air, the Pire, the Water. They all had to be kept pure. And so you find that the Parsī in modern India, the descendant of the Perso-Āryans, will not bury his dead, because that would pollute the Earth; he will not burn his dead, because that would pollute the Fire; he will not put his dead into the rivers, because that would pollute the Water. And that purity of the elements is a very remarkable step forward in human thought. That was the great contribution of Persia, which as you know made a mighty Empire, as Egypt had done before it, and that thought survives.

In every sub-race you have two Beings, the Lawgiver and the Teacher of the Religion. The Law-giver makes a polity, an outer civilisation, a framework for the

20

Nation. The Teacher gives the religion which works in with that polity, develops it, strengthens it, limits it or enlarges it.

And then you come to the next emigration, third emigration, or fourth sub-race, the Indo-Keltic. That had the dominant note of Beauty. The "beauty that was Greece," as they say. Art was its great characteristic. The beauty of painting, the beauty of sculpture, the beauty of architecture, and also the beauty of language, in which it embodied its thoughts in its literature, a wonderful language, a flexible language, a language full of music to the ear, as well as able to express the minute diversities of thought. And the Latin Nations, as they are called, show out that beauty, for they have descended from this fourth sub-race, the Keltic, and the French, Spanish, and Italian languages still show this in their music and accuracy. Beauty, remember, is a great emotion, and that third emigration developed the emotional qualities of the human being, for emotion dominated, however it showed itself forth, as you still find in the southern or Latin Nations of Europe, as well in the northern Kelts—the southern Irish, or the Highland Scotch.

And then came next the Teutonic, in order to develop the concrete mind. You see we are following the same order. That is what makes this comparatively easy to understand in all its complexity, if you have once grasped the dominating principle. These sub-races develop one by one these characteristics of human beings, so adding more and more to the great store of man. And when you come to what was the fourth emigration,, the fifth sub-race, then you have the development of that scientific, concrete mind which you see in this Teutonic sub-race, whether you call them Teutons—though that is not a popular name to-day—or whether you call them English, because they are both of the same stock, or Americans, or your Self-governing Dominions in their white races. It is a sub-race marked by the activity of this concrete mind, and showing itself forth mostly in science and its practical applications, in organisation and self-discipline, with an overwhelming sense of the value of individuality. And all these things have been developing one after another, until we get the human beings of to-day, with these types developed in them, each with one dominating faculty. And it is this dominating faculty which makes the great difference between the Kelt and the Teuton, with results which are going on at the present time within the limits of this one Kingdom. They cannot understand each other. They are two different types; different sub-races, with different ways of looking at the world; and until they learn to sympathise, instead of quarrelling, they cannot find a really true union. It is not the fault of either side, but the fundamental differences of the human temperament are in the way. And so we come to where we are now, in our fourth and fifth sub-races.

But, you say, you have left out the Root-Stock. The remarkable point about that is that that shows out in itself at different stages of its own growth resemblances of the succession of sub-races born of it, and it is the only one of the great civilisations of antiquity that still endures—a thing to remember when we are coming to our next two lectures. For you have to remember that India was a mighty, civilised power, trading, colonising, enormously wealthy, with a wonderful and varied literature, when she traded with Babylon 3000 years before the Christian Era, and she came down all through the millennia, still showing out these wonderful capacities and varied powers of mind. She was philosophical, she was political, she tried every form of political government that has since been tried in the daughter sub-races. In the time of Alexander, in the fourth century before the

Christian Era, there were fourteen Schools of Political Science[1]—I mean by Schools, not buildings, but types of thought—existing in India, discussing, quarrelling, and agreeing ; working themselves out sometimes in Republics, sometimes in City States like those of Greece, sometimes in Council Governments, sometimes in Royal Governments and sometimes in Imperial Governments, and so on, an extraordinary mass of political experiments and of knowledge developed from these. Most of you know India vaguely as philosophical, you know her as metaphysical, you know her as religious, but very few of you know her as political. And yet her experiments in political life have been fat' more numerous than those of other Nations, because her life is so much longer, a Nation that has had—to say the very least of it—a civilisation for at least 5000 years, as great and as complex as that of Babylon—a remarkable phenomenon, because all the daughter civilisations have perished, and the present one is perishing, broken into pieces.

If you realise that we have come to that stage, you will see what I mean by the phrase "The World's Opportunity". We have come, as it were, to the point in the development of the concrete mind where other lines of thought and other methods of thought have to be taken up. The next stage beyond the mind which was the separating force, is that of the uniting, the union.

I ought to have said—I forgot it at the moment in speaking of the Lawgiver and the Teacher—it is a peculiarity of Christianity, which was given for the special development of the individual, that no polity was given with that which was distinctly Christianity. In all other cases they work together, but in the develop-ment of the individual, which was the work of Christianity—the value of the individual, the strength of the individual, the combativeness of the individual which inevitably grew out of it, in order that strength might be developed—there was no definite Lawgiver with a political plan put on Christendom, but only a religion given by the great Teacher, the Christ. He gave the religion, and it was to work itself out in all its wonderful variety, just because it was specifically an individualising faith, and that was why it lost reincarnation ; that doctrine was taught in many different forms in the early Church, and then it was banned in the form adopted by Origen by a Church Council.

Reincarnation diminishes the value of the individual, the value of the individual life. You always have another chance, you always have another opportunity. You may have failed, but you say: "I shall have another life, and I will succeed." You may have broken down, but you say: "I shall have another life, and I will stand up." It lessens the value of the individual life. Whereas to drop reincarnation out of religion, and to make the everlasting future of the man depend on the way in which he lives or believes in this one brief mortal life, gave an enormous strength to the development of the individual. This life was like a lifeboat in a storm, on which all the lives of the sailors depend; the whole life of the man depended on his single earth-life; everlasting happiness, everlasting misery, turned on these few years of mortal life. Not a very rational view, I grant, but a necessary view for development (for reasons you will see in the later lectures), where another view of the relations of human beings had to be taken.

And the world's opportunity lies in this, that we are now at the transition stage

---

[1] See *Ārthashāstra* of Chānakya (Kautilya).

of human evolution, of racial evolution, in which the next step forward, according to the ladder that was descended and that we are ascending, is Union, and not persistence in division.

You may not have thought, when I began, that I was coming to that conclusion. I wanted it to rest on a definite and reasoned basis. For there are being born to-day in all parts of the world, and most largely in America, a new type of men, not that which is concerned with the individualising mind but with the Life, which is thinning and lessening the walls, trying to unite itself with the life in others that once more it may be one. And if you look at the records in the Washington Bureau of Ethnology, you may find traced out the physical characteristics of this new type. They call it American; that does not matter; there are more of them in America, and so they have drawn more attention, but there are many in other countries; they are being born in different parts of the world, this same type, recognisable and distinguishable from the ordinary multitude by their similarities. It means a new departure. It means another quality is coming out now, and that the cultivation of human individuality has done its work, and that the civilisation which embodied individuality is breaking into pieces all around us, because it naturally has its end in combat and war, with war between Nation and Nation, combat between class and class within the limit of a Nation. And if you look abroad you will see signs of a desire for more union, signs of aspiration for a more human life, signs of a longing that within a Nation classes shall unite and form a real family, instead of being warring fragments as they are unhappily at the present time. And whether by success or failure in the struggles between classes, one thing is sure, that they will find that union and co-operation are better than division and combat, and that to work for a common end is more important than the pressing of the interests of a particular individual or a class of individuals. Whether by pain or by necessity, the world is being pushed in that direction. It may resist, and reap still much fruit of misery; but if wisdom is chosen, it will recognise its opportunity, marked by its place in evolution; it will then work for Union, for an ever wider and wider circle of Union, class united with class, and Nation with Nation, and later, Humanity in one great Unity in the far, far future that is before us, that our study may forecast with certainty. Everything that tends to Union now is on the line of evolution, and everything that tends to separation is on the line of the past which we ought to have outgrown; and the great difference in the coming years—that to which I hope to lead you in the next two lectures—is that we have before us now in this land of Great Britain a possibility—if we can take it up and carry it out—of making a model for the future Federation of the World. The world is not yet ripe, because of the great differences between the Races, to join them all together in the perfect Federation. But it is possible here, where there are links, which have been bonds of Empire and shall become links of Commonwealth, if you can bring about Union, Union between India and Britain, between East and West, between Asia and Europe. For that reason were India and Britain brought together, that they might unite the elder and the younger races in a Commonwealth of Free Nations, where all shall stand together, linked by amity, friendship, mutual respect, mutual support, mutual service, equally free, equal in status, the first great conglomeration of peoples brought together, not in an Empire made by force, but in a Commonwealth made by mutual goodwill and friendliness. That is the great opportunity of Britain and India to-day, and that will be the model for the World's Federation in the future.

Lecture III
The Conflict of East and West

FRIENDS: We have arrived to-night at what I may call the more concrete part of the subject on which these four talks are being delivered. In the first lecture, you may remember, I carried you far away into regions not very closely thought over as a rule, dealing with the Inner Government of the World. Last Sunday I tried to put before you the methods of that Government, and to suggest a great opportunity that lay before the world of building a civilisation on securer, on more permanent, lines.

To-day, I have as title "The Conflict of East and West". Sometimes I am inclined to think that here in the West you almost forget that there is an East, throbbing with life, throbbing with energy, full of aspirations, full of hopes; and an East, moreover, that has behind it—especially in the country most closely connected with yourselves—a past so immense in its length, so complicated in its details, that one wonders almost, living there, as I of course do, why Great Britain does not take more interest in India, and see whether it may not be possible, looking at the two civilisations so different in their character, it may not be possible to build a mightier civilisation by blending the ideals, the two being at first sight opposed but really complementary the one to the other. For the length of Indian history is a phenomenon unique in history—and I will come to that in a moment, when I remind you that the first conflicts, as it were, between East and West one can pass over very swiftly, for they were physical, not a conflict of Ideals but a conflict of Nations. Europe invaded by Asia and Asia invaded by Europe; the pendulum of power swinging from one side to the other.

Not very long ago, in India, I read an English review, or rather an English book, which remarked, for the first time I had seen it in an English book, on this swing of the pendulum between these two great divisions, the great continents of Asia and Europe. And the writer said—a rather surprising statement, coming as it did from a Westerner—that the pendulum was now swinging towards Asia, suggesting a dominance of eastern ideals and of eastern power.

Each of these great invasions of one continent by the other has left its traces behind; and it is not easy to decide which of the two has left its mark more deeply on the other. Sometimes we forget, in the case of war, in the case of invasions, that they have an aftermath of benefit to both countries or to both continents. When Alexander invaded India, although his stay was not long there, still Greek influence existed over a considerable period; and you cannot but notice the influence of Greek art on Indian art, the effects that you find in statues, the effects that you find in carvings of various kinds, the Greek type coming out, and almost, in some parts of the country, overbearing the purely Asiatic. And if you look for the swing on the other way, then you cannot but notice that when the learning came from Arabia and was carried by the Moors into southern Europe and into Spain, it was one of the results of that invasion, of that settling, that science revived again in Europe, and began its great struggle against the Roman Catholic Church, being accused first as a form of sorcery; and even a Roman Pope, Sylvester the Second, I think it was, because he used compasses and drew some of the propositions of Euclid, was said by the "wise" men around him to be practising magic and to be having dealings with the devil. Still, despite that opposition, science made its way, and the darkness that followed on the fall of Rome was finally dispelled by the advance of science, and Europe took up again, after a thousand years of darkness, science where it had been left in Greece and in Egypt.

And so, if you look at philosophy instead of science, you find how in southern Italy the memories of Pythagoras had survived, and the school of Pythagoras had left its traces even in the monasteries of the Middle Ages; and we remember that Pythagoras drew his teachings from Egypt and then from India, so that from the far East and from the middle East there came that great Greek philosophy which moulded all the thought of Europe, stamping itself deeply into the minds of the people. But the greatest influence that has been exercised over Europe by Asiatic ideals is, of course, the influence of the great religion of the Christ. Sometimes it almost seems to one, looking over the world to-day, as though that world, so far as it is Christian, had well-nigh forgotten that the Lord Christ was Himself an Asiatic, belonging to the Hebrew race, coming from Palestine. The Christian Bible, the Old Testament, is an Asiatic book, as indeed is the New Testament also. And yet in the white countries we find that the Asiatic is barred and is despised; so that if we borrow a thought from Stead, my old friend, who wrote *If Christ came to Chicago,* we might try to imagine what would happen in our time if Christ, the coloured Asiatic, went to South Africa, or to East Africa, or to Australia, or to New Zealand, or to Canada. The Asiatic is worshipped in a far-away Heaven—he is despised when in this world; he goes into countries marked by Nature for the coloured man, and finds they are to be guarded as white countries for the Europeans. And so, looking at this, we wonder how far the real influence has gone, even of so mighty a Teacher as the Christ Himself. And we wonder if He should come again, "If Christ came to South Africa," what welcome He would find in those who use His Name as theirs?

Looking thus hastily over these changes, alike in the physical world of Nations and in the ideal world of thought and emotion, which are held up by the various Nations as goals towards which they strive, we begin to wonder a little whether this opposition is always to continue; whether part of that Great Plan, of which I spoke in my first lecture, may not include, by the union of Great Britain and India, a blending of the ideals into a greater Ideal of the Future, when each shall learn from each and shall take that which is good from the other, while preserving that which each has worked out as good for itself.

Looking now for a moment at India, I said it was unique in the length of its history. That length from the European standpoint is indeterminate. No ordinary historian here would venture to give a date when the Indo-Aryan came down from Asia after the great emigrations had gone out from the Root-Stock, had civilised Egypt, parts of Africa, and the borders of the Mediterranean; had made a great Empire in Persia and had then gone further westwards to Greece, to Rome, building the Latin Nations of Europe; and the last of those great emigrations to northern Europe, building up the Teutonic sub-race, including, of course, the Briton, as coming from the Anglo-Saxon tribes, or whatever is the most modern name for this particular set of people, carrying with them, as Maine pointed out, the great Aryan traditions of freedom and self-government from their eastern home.

If you turn aside from ordinary western history for the moment, you find suggestions, when Plato writes of what the Egyptians told him when he was passing through the Egyptian Initiation into the Mysteries, and how they spoke of the great island Poseidonis, which is recognised now as an eastern part of the great continent of Atlantis, the last of that to survive so far as the western world is concerned.

It is said that the Indo-Āryans came down into India across Kashmir and Baluchistan and Assam, where passes existed for their passage came down about 9000 B.C., shortly before that tremendous earthquake that caused, and the tidal wave that followed on, the ruin, the destruction that Plato speaks of as falling upon Poseidonis; but it does not particularly matter, nine thousand years more or less will not really affect the point that I want to put to you. A great German scholar says that the religious literature of the Indo-Āryans, the Vedas, cannot be younger than five thousand years before the time of Christ, the Christian Era. And we come across touches of this very ancient India when it comes into contact with other civilisations of which somewhat more is known, thanks to the researches of modern antiquarians and archaeologists. And so we get a number of dates that would not be challenged now by anyone who has studied the subject at all; for we find, for instance, ancient Babylon, three thousand years before the Christian Era; India traded with that mighty civilisation, pre-Āryan civilisation, and was a wealthy, a prosperous, a highly civilised country; and that is nearly five thousand years ago from our time. Then a thousand years later, two thousand years before the Christian Era—and how long before that none may say,—we find Egyptian mummies which were swathed in the fine muslins of India, which still were made millennium after millennium—one of the things which attracted in 1600 the English merchants to gain a charter from Queen Elizabeth for trading with the East Indies. Then, coming a little further down, you find also that she is in very close contact with the great Empire of Persia, and that Sindh and part of Panjab paid to Darius of Persia huge tribute in gold year by year. And then we find India trading with Greece in more modern times, and with Rome, Imperial Rome. We find Pliny (vide *India a Nation*, p. 14) complaining that the Roman ladies of the Imperial Court clothed themselves in Indian silks and wasted very, very much gold on these Indian manufactures. And so on and on I might take you, century after century, millennium after millennium; and the whole of these things go to show this one fact, that this India was a great trading, a great commercial, a great colonising, and a great shipbuilding Nation through these enormous periods of time; wealthy and prosperous; so wealthy that she attracted the eyes of greedy Central Asian and European Nations, that they might share in that wealth. And coming down through Indian history, it is recognised by all, as you may read if you will in a valuable book by Vincent Smith, that that India of the older time had every kind of political experiment tried on her soil.

You think of India as a great philosophical country with her own metaphysical literature; a great metaphysical and religious country; and you know most of the translations that have been made of that line of thought in India. You hardly realise that for hundreds upon hundreds of years—nay! for thousands—she was trying every form of political organisation known in the history of the world. You find there Republics, flourishing and strong; States governed by Councils; you find limited and absolute Monarchies; Ministers making Kings and Peoples electing Kings. You find City States, like the City State of Aristotle. And you find mighty Empires, like the Empire Chandragupta Maurya I. organised, perfectly organised in all the details of what you might think a modern Goverment, with its registration of births and deaths, with its army and its navy, its municipal Governments, its various Councils elected by the people, and the whole of them based on the villages, which were the unit of government through all these thousands of years.

Or, if you take the Empire of his grandson Ashoka, you find it stretching from the Hindu Khush right down to what is now Madras ; and you find Viceroys there—not only one Viceroy, as in modern times, but four Viceroys—through whom that great Empire was administered; Ashoka, of course, the fifth, over them all.

If you went further East you would find her colonies clearly traceable to-day by the marks of her civilisation and her religion in Java, in Sumatra, and in neighbouring islands. So that you gradually realise that you are face to face here with a civilisation marvellous for its length and its prosperity, for its wealth and its political institutions; and surely such a civilisation, lasting so long, so wealthy, so prosperous and so strong, must have had something to explain that long prosperity, something that it may have to suggest to the modern civilisation over here, something that may be of use and of value in the ideals that there were followed and realised, and that kept it secure and stable for a period of time that would seem a dream, if we did not see it touching civilisation after civilisation, always strong and rich, and itself civilised right down to the eighteenth century. India must surely have something to give to you politically.

I take first, however, the religious side, for every great Teacher of religion that the world has known is an Asiatic, and that must mean something for the world. Not one has been born out of Asia; and a vast continent that has thus given to the world Those who are more revered than any monarch, more revered than any conqueror, Those who are crowned with the love, the adoration of Humanity— whether you take the Lord Buddha or the Lord Christ—surely such a continent has something worth hearing by the West; something to say which may be of use in trying to outline our ideals of the future, the rebuilding of civilisation out of the fragments that lie around us to-day.

So let us for a moment glance, not at the detail which touches your modern problems—that I keep for next Sunday—but at the great Ideals which underlie the civilisations of the East and of the West. For it is these big Ideals which mould the thoughts and hearts of men. It is these which really make a civilisation, however important the economic aspect of it may be, or the political aspect of it may be; there is something that is greater than the outer organisation, and that is the Ideals which mould the brains and the hearts of the people, and which gradually civilise and train and uplift.

Now, what are the Ideals of the East as opposed, for the moment, to the Ideals of the West? You must remember that, when we speak in this sense of the East, we speak of India, for India has dominated the civilisation of Asia. If you look at Japan, they tell you that they draw from India their civilisation. If you look at China, you find there the multitudes who bow before the Lord Buddha. The great mystic Lao-tsze, the great philosopher Confucius, appeal more to the learned among the Chinese; and very splendid are their sayings and their thoughts. But Buddhism spread upwards, northwards from India, passed through Tibet, went on into China, so that some of the most splendid of the Lord Buddha's teachings come to us in Chinese garb and are translated from the Chinese into our own tongue, profoundly interesting when put side by side with those that came from the Pāli—more familiar over here than those that are drawn from the Chinese recensions of His teachings,—on some points differing considerably, although the outline of the morality is identical. But in the Chinese, more of philosophy than as yet has made very much impression, I think, in Great Britain, although in the Pāli you find the philosophy differs on one great point from that which we find in China. Putting it roughly, I would say that China has remembered that the Lord Buddha was a Hindu, and took some of the essential truths of the great spiritual verities for granted, speaking to Hindus from the Hindu view of truth; and that is found more in the recensions that come from China than from those that come from Ceylon, from Burma, and from Siam. But it is not that difference that I have aught to do with really this evening.

It is interesting, as regards the Lord Buddha Himself, that He lived surrounded largely by Republics, and based His own great Order and the government of His Order on the Council Government that He found in the Republics; so that, when in that Order some new law is to be promulgated and His directions, as exist in the books, are carried out, we find, in what we may call the great Buddhic Parliament, political method is used in a religious assembly, and that when the law is proposed it is put to the vote by acclamation; if any dissent in that, it is argued and put again the second time, and still unanimity is sought for; and if for the third time after discussion unanimity is not found, then they proceed to the voting, in the way they did in Lord Buddha's day when they voted in the political Councils, with little slips of wood, one coloured for "Yes" and one for "No". Sometimes a secret ballot, if they wished it, and sometimes open voting. And it may be well just to bear that in mind, because it may get out of your minds the idea that these things are not familiar by tradition and by practice right down through Hindu history.

Now as to these ideals: What is the profound difference between them? In India the human being is regarded as "the man, the wife, and the child". None of the three is complete by him or herself. The Hindu scriptures have it: "God created men to be fathers and women to be mothers," and the ideal human being is therefore defined in one of the great books of the law as "the man, the wife, and the child". The family is the unit, not the individual. And this has profound and far-reaching results. The family has grown in India into what is called the joint family. That is to say, that the father and the mother and the sons and their wives form an ever-increasing family, the daughters becoming part of the family of their husbands; and in these joint families, which still exist down to the present day and stretch backwards far into the night of time, there is practically scarcely any distinction between the children of the family, so far as regards fathers or uncles; they are all one family; with the result that among the Hindus has grown up a sense of community that you do not find here in the West, where the married couple go out to make a separate home, a home of their own, separate from the parents. And all through this joint family there is common property belonging to the home, and the elder the trustee of that property; and, looking back to the village life, you see how naturally that grew up in those villages, which are the units of government in India, made naturally out of families and allied families. That has gone on, as I said, right down to the present day, but it is gradually breaking up. Individualism is asserting itself there as it has long asserted itself in Europe, so that the joint family is becoming less common, although in that huge population of India you find it up and down among the more orthodox Indians. There is a tendency to break away from it, and the result of that presumably will be to loosen the bonds of the family. One effect it had was that you did not have the terrible poverty that you have where individualism has swayed the people as an ideal, for the old people were inevitably nourished and guarded and cared for in the joint home; the children, they also were educated and trained and supported in the joint home. And this strong family tie influenced the whole life of India, first in making general the community ideal, which was the ideal of the village, and then in making the whole State largely communal, with the inevitable results that I will speak of next week in the questions of holding land, crafts, and so on.

Now what comes out of that ideal when you look at it from the moral standpoint? Clearly the sense of Duty, the sense of Obligation. Where you take a family, elders, contemporaries, and youngers, the success of the family or its destruction rests on the discharge of the mutual family duties and obligations. In India it has not been the way to look upon man as born free, because to the logical mind of the Hindu a baby left free and untended, without others performing duties and owing obligations to it, would have a remarkably small chance of surviving into boyhood or girlhood or maturity, for the baby is a helpless creature when born into the world. And the whole result of recognising that fact, and looking on the family as a unit in the State, gradually transferred the idea of duty and obligation within the family to duties and obligations of the citizens to the State. That is the dominant note in India: Duty. They have their own word for it, an untranslatable word: DHARMA. And the whole civilisation is practically worked out on the basis of the family. If you take the duties which grow out of the family tie, the tie of blood, and the affection which grows up in the family from duties rendered by each to each, you have there in love the real bond between elders and contemporaries and youngers, with the recognition of the various duties which each owes to all. And if you take that family idea which knows no law, since "love is the fulfilling of the law," and if you extend the family idea to all the members of the Community or of the State, if you see them as elders, contemporaries, and youngers, and duties belonging to each grade in life, you then pass on to what was the original of the Caste ideal, not as it is to-day, a matter of pride, of oppression, but as it was in the days when it was founded, and founded on the ideal of the family. For you have there—and the thought has come back again in Ruskin—the recognition of the functions in every Nation, without which a Nation cannot exist; you have the citizens of the State with their duties to the State, the functions which they discharge, so that all the functions of the individual become part of a National Service; and in this great division of the Castes—which was into Brain-Workers, Rulers, Organisers and Distributors, or Merchants, and Producers of wealth—you have there the four great functions of National life, each equally sacred as a function discharged to the whole, not simply an individual gaining his livelihood, but a citizen performing a certain part as an organ in the National life. And as long as they went by qualities, as long as each type of human being passed into his appropriate discharge of function as marked out by his capacities, so long the organisation was fruitful of good to the State; but when it passed into being a mere matter of birth, when it became purely hereditary, when into the Caste of Brain-Workers someone might be born who had no high intellect, who was not a scientist, or philosopher, or teacher of religion, or teacher in the schools or colleges or universities, but had capacities quite other, fitting him for other work, then it was that Caste confusion arose, because capacity no longer marked out the function to be discharged in the Nation; it became a hereditary matter, and those who were born into a particular family need not have any necessary power or capacity for the Caste to which they nominally belonged. And so you had the destruction practically of the system, for the life went out of it. While the life was in it, and every citizen of the State was himself discharging a National Service and not simply gaining a livelihood, then it worked well and gave great stability to the social system. How that might be brought into modern life without the rigidity which ruined it, and ruins it still in India; when it shall be made dependent on the faculties as shown in the educational period, marking the avocation into which a boy or a girl should pass—then in the fulness of time you will have what was good and avoid what was evil in that system. And that some of the great thinkers of our own time have seen. Ruskin was one; Auguste Comte was another; but he brought in the hereditary principle, and made it even more hopeless as an organisation of the State.

Now, looking for a moment at those family duties that I spoke of, externalise them to the Nation, make them universal, make them to be rendered by all and made permanent, and you have the social virtues. When you realise duties, when you realise that the nature of the duties depends on your own faculties and on the faculties of those around you, then you begin to realise what it means when it is said that "love is the fulfilling of the law". For in that family emotion when rendered universal and rendered permanent as a part of the character, you have, instead of emotion, virtue, all the virtues that grow out of love. And that has been admirably shown by an Indian writer, Bhagavan Das, who pointed out that out of the emotion of love, made permanent in the character, all virtues grow; out of the emotion of hate rendered permanent, all vices develop; and for the first time, I think, these foundations of virtues and vices were shown clearly and definitely by him, one of the outcomes of modern Indian thought, valuable when you are dealing with the building up of a civilisation. Let us then take, as we well may, because there is no challenge on this point, that the great idea, the ruling Ideal of India, lies in the discharge of duty and the obligations between members of a Community or a Nation.

Now when you look at Greece and Rome, they come, as it were, half-way between Asia and Europe, influenced by Asia certainly and then influencing Europe; you have a peculiar change in the family, and the State becomes purely masculine. This comes out in Aristotle. He says that everyone who is a citizen of a State must be capable of fulfilling any office in the State; and he took it for granted that there were a large number of offices in the State, in fact practically all of them, that could not be filled except by men; and so no one but a man could be a citizen in his City State. That again influenced Rome very largely, with the addition of the tremendous power given to the father of the family—the power of life and death over his sons. And curiously that purely masculine ideal was revived in modern Germany in its Ideal of the State. If you take a well-known writer, Bluntschli, you find him declaring that the State must be masculine, and he argues in his book on the line of the pure masculinity of the State. That has probably passed out of State ideals by the war. Passing from Greece and Rome, on which I need not dwell, you come to the modern idea—I call it modern although you have just to look for a moment at your Anglo-Saxon forefathers, whose Village System was practically the same as the Indian, and you find there the same arrangement of the Villages; they brought it from Central Asia, and on that English liberty is founded. The unwritten laws of England, the unwritten Constitution of England, those are based entirely on that great Village System in England, when the Teutonic people came over and brought it with them. And that unwritten law and Constitution is what has been picked out from time to time in history, as in the Magna Carta, in the Bill of Rights—before all Statutes, before all Parliaments, the inalienable right of the Āryans to life, to liberty, and to property, and on that is based the great Liberty of this country; that Liberty that England has held up as an ideal in the past, and to which if she is false to-day she seals her own doom, for she has been Liberty's standard-bearer among all the Nations of the world, and has made Liberty synonymous with her name.

And now we come to the ideal of that, so different from the ideal of the East; it is the Ideal of Individuality—the individual. Now that is a necessary ideal. Without the strong individual you could not take the next step onwards, the next great step in civilisation. For you can no more build a house without bricks or stones, than you can build a lasting civilisation in which the sense of individuality had not been developed. Now that is based on Christianity. Christianity was the first religion in the world that laid tremendous stress on the value of the individual. The other religions, like the polities founded on them, always took as unit the family, never the individual; and that is the peculiar value of Christianity to the world—it brought out the sense of individuality and its value. It has worked much harm on its way, for that is but one of the two great ideals of Christianity; the other one was the Ideal of Service. After strength had been developed, after strength had proved itself, then strength was to be used for service and not for oppression; that was the second point. Now the first was connected with the development of the concrete mind. You remember that I pointed out to you how these various capacities in the human being were evolved one after another in the long course of evolution; and just as emotion and art and the love of beauty were the special evolution of the Keltic sub-race, or the Latin races, whichever you choose to call them—Greeks, Romans, southern European peoples—just as emotion was the mark of the Kelt and is the mark of the Kelt to-day, so the concrete mind was the mark of the Teuton—the German. Teuton is a better name, because Germany is only one part of the Teutonic sub-race, and Scandinavians and Britons, all these belong to that great sub-race, and in them you find the high development of the concrete mind. Science is its mark; the immense development of science among these people of the Teutonic sub-race is due to that development of the lower mind in man which works by observation, by reasoning, by argument, by logic, caring less for the beauty of expression than for the depth and the strength and the logical character of the thought. The profound difference between the two sub-races, Kelts and Teutons, is one reason of the constant misunderstandings that you find between England and Ireland, members of those two sub-races, the one moved by emotion, the other by reasoning, the one full of impulse and the other more cautious and more logical. Looking at this—this development of the concrete mind, with the tremendous sense of its own rights, its own individuality—you come to the more modern phase of thought, where you have the individual clothed with his rights as the unit in the State. They talk of course about the contract, the social contract, that everybody knows never took place, and is only a word used in order to explain a certain relationship between human beings, that each has his own rights inalienable and born in him, rights that he may properly assert against all corners, the inherent liberty of man—a profound truth, although veiled in so much of error and for so long.

Now in Christianity two great doctrines disappeared which had existed everywhere in the elder civilisations of the East. I mentioned them in my first lecture—the doctrine of Karma, or cause and effect, universal causation; and the doctrine of Reincarnation, the individual life prolonged, dwelling in one body after another, passing innumerable times through birth and death, and bringing with it into each successive birth the results of past struggles and past failures, as explained last week. These underlaid the whole of the thoughts of the East, and do still. The doctrine of reincarnation, that, as already said, had been taught in various forms in the early Church and by the early Church Fathers, was banned by the Church in the sixth century, I think it was, and so it vanished for a time from the Christian world, except among heretics, among the Albigenses and others. That was a necessary loss of a great truth, because the doctrine of reincarnation does, as already pointed out, diminish the value of each separate individual human life. If you have not done it in this life, you will do it in another; if you have missed your chances here, you will grasp them in another.

The doctrine is coming back again now that the strength of the individual is well established in the western world. It is re-emerging because of its eminent rationality, because of its obvious applicability to the varying capacities of men. At the time it was obscured in order that the individual might grow into strength and power. Now inevitably that led to much of conflict, not only of Nation against Nation, but of class against class, of man against man, and so you had the great struggles that you find in Europe. The individual claimed his own right: "Let the best man win"; it is a very popular axiom still, but that means anarchy. "Let the best man serve" is the truth, and that means ordered progress. And that is the second great ideal of Christianity. It was that on which the Christ laid such immense stress. "Let him that is greatest among you, be as he that doth serve. Behold, I am among you as he that serveth." And so again in the writings of one of His great Apostles you find that supreme truth in the example of the Christ: "Though He were rich, yet for our sakes He became poor, that we by His poverty might become rich". There you have the doctrine of Human Brotherhood, the doctrine of human sacrifice, put in a single sentence, embodied in a superhuman life. And that second great ideal, following, as it did follow in the course of evolution, on the unbounded strength of the individual and his grasping, with the resultant anarchy, has now to come to the front as the dominating part of one of our great ideals of the future. That is the greatest contribution that Christianity has made to the world, not an enforced sacrifice, but a voluntary sacrifice, the sweeping down of the high to lift up the lowly, and the using of all strength for helping the weak.

Now much has been done in Britain to emphasise that truth, and there is one point I would like to put to you, because I know it is one as to which a very great and not wholly unfair attack is made on the great combinations of manual workers here—a groping after a very great truth, but crude in its expression, and so easily twisted and shown to be absurd and mischievous. For it is put in a very crude

32

form—that the best workman shall limit his skill, his work, his production, so as not to outdo his weaker brother, whose capacity and skill are less. Now that is the doctrine which has been more attacked perhaps than any other in Trade Unionism; and naturally so, put in that very crude form, for people see that it diminishes production and thus injures the Nation. "You are making a certain arrangement for helping certain brothers in your Union, but you are injuring your Nation by diminishing your own productive power"; and, put in that way, it is difficult to defend. But if you can see what underlies it, if you can see into the dim gropings of minds which have caught a glimpse of the beauty of Brotherhood and are trying to realise it in the family sense, in which the younger is not crushed because his capacities are less or his strength is smaller, but rather helped and cherished by his elders because he is yet young, and not able to fight for himself in the battle of life; if you can see that in that there is a sense of a larger Self that has to be served above the smaller Self, then you will realise that they are groping after a mighty truth, only the way in which it is put is crude and unwise. And it is as well sometimes to look at a thing that you do not like from its better side and not from its worse, to try to see the motive of the people who make a rule that seems at first so mischievous, so restrictive; and you can only do it by, as it were, trying to get into their hearts and minds, and thus see at what they are really aiming. Then you will begin to realise that just because that feeling of brotherhood has grown up among the manual workers in the country, that Britain is perhaps almost the only country which can make the great transition into a higher civilisation without a revolution which shall whelm the Nation in disaster. It is just that realisation that everyone is part of a larger Self, whose interests have to be thought of, a Self that has to be expanded and has to embrace the Nation and not a particular craft only, which is true; so that you will not have certain bodies of workers set over, as it were, against the Nation, striving to impose their will upon it by the power of numbers and of the National life which they hold in their hands, but you will have an organised Nation, in which everyone will have his place, everyone will have his work, will have his own function to discharge. Then we may realise that this is really what we are striving after, to understand how to reconcile the claims of the Nation and the claims of the individual, the family Ideal of the East and the individualistic Ideal of the West.

For, have not Britain and India something to learn of each other, as I suggested in the beginning? And may we not find next week, in looking more into the detail, that each has something to teach the other, each has something to give? That in this age-long evolution towards different Ideals each has gone to excess along its own particular line, and needs to be corrected by the other? That the Ideal of the family carried to excess has led to too much submission, too much subservience, too much erasing of the individual, too little care for liberty? But India has been learning and assimilating the Ideal of the West more rapidly than the West is inclined to learn and assimilate the Ideal of the East. For India has caught from you your sense of liberty, your feeling of the value of the individual, your realisa- tion that a Nation to be really great must be free throughout; and that this is to be won, not—if it may be—by conflict, but by mutual understanding and sympathy and desire to serve. And so it is that in these Ideals, which seem to be so contrary, we may find in each the corrective of the other; that we have to blend together the liberty of the individual and also the welfare of the Nation, that the Nation is a family on a larger scale, a greater Self, to which the smaller selves must conform themselves; that we may find after all that in these two Nations, one the great elder of the East, the other inspiring and largely guiding the West, that they have been brought up apart, that they have been developed separately, that their religions have been different, in order that the two great Ideals might be gradually evolved throughout the ages, and then brought together, then bound together, then united, different as they are; that we may find the blending of two great Ideals, the joining together of two necessary views of human life, and so may find a reconciliation, not for these two great countries only, but for the whole of Humanity.

Then it shall be realised that men live not for themselves but for all, that even Nations exist not for themselves but for all the other Nations together; and from these ideals of family and of individuality we may find a yet higher Ideal, in which each shall take its place, and that shall form in turn a platform on which a still mightier Ideal shall lift itself—that great Ideal of Nations as one Family, the Ideal of Universal Peace.

Lecture IV
The Ideal of the Future

FRIENDS: In reading a newspaper to-day I found a very interesting lecture by Sir Michael Sadler, who is apparently very largely in his thought as to the reorganisation of Society running along the line on which I have been trying to lead you in the last three weeks. He points out—he is speaking at Mirfield, opening some buildings for a new Community—he points out that modern civilisation is a colossal fact, and then goes on to say that this modern civilisation has been achieved by the courage and labour of western men during four centuries. It is obvious from the context and from looking back that he is really starting with the sixteenth century, after the Wars of the Roses, and passing on through the seventeenth, eighteenth, and nineteenth. Then he says that through these centuries "the great characteristic, the essence, of Western Civilisation, was Power. Its phases had been: the power of the individual Pioneer; the power of the State; the power of the Sea; the power of the Machine; the power of Coal; and the power of High Explosives". And through this stupendous outburst of Power, Providence had permitted a great change in the minds of men all over the world. Then he goes on to say:

In the heart and conscience of modern civilisation there is now foreboding. Power, which is the essence of modern civilisation, threatens to destroy it. Three men as typical as Viscount Grey, Mr. H. G. Wells, and the Dean of S. Paul's, warn us that modern civilisation is at the cross-roads of its destiny. Unless by some deflection of its recent purpose, Power can be concentrated upon the constructive works of Peace, it will destroy civilisation by War.

Then he goes on to point out that just at this moment there is a certain tendency to turn back, with "some amount of wistfulness," he calls it, to medieval times; and he slightly elaborates that thesis, and shows how in Industry there has been some revival of the Mediæval Guild, how in Art a similar change has shown itself, how in Politics the Nations are looking to a Council of Peoples, and are recognising Nationhood but trying to allay its rivalries. And alluding to Matthew Arnold, he says that he felt in himself the attractions of the Middle Ages as a Past, but that instead of that "men are looking at a possible revival drawn from it as the dawn of a new era". And finally he goes on to say that history cannot repeat itself, but that though we cannot go back to the Middle Ages and become mediæval in our thought and way of life, it is possible that

the future may blend some mediæval ideas with those derived from the age of Power, and that what is perilous in some modern tendencies may be transmuted by a re-discovery of some aspects of Mediæval Life into an improvement of the present condition. All honour to those who, while bravely modern in spirit, are willing to learn from and to practise what was best in the Mediæval way of life.

And he mentions three Powers that, he says, then worked in harmony in the life of Christendom; they were: the Priesthood, the Empire, and the University; "For all three, in a form adapted to modern needs, the modern world may find a place".

Now under that conception there lies, I think, a profound truth. I should go much further back than the Mediæval Age. It is, I think, the tendency only of the modern European mind which stops within the boundaries of Europe and the age of Europe and refuses to go further East, where civilisations endured for so much longer periods, periods of which it would not be unfair to say that some aspects of Mediæval Europe were the reproduction of the further East. I mentioned to you, I think, in one of my lectures, in speaking of the East, that Europeans always look back only as far as Aristotle, except Maine, who saw that Humanity had had a much longer experience before Aristotle was born than since his time, and desired to trace much of modern Europe right back to the immemorial traditions of India and her organisation for the individual and the State. To-night I am going to try to draw out some of those ancient ideals, which, blended with our modern ideals, may give us an Ideal for the immediate Future. Not for the very, very far-off future, for Nations, like individuals, cannot proceed by immense leaps, immense changes in human nature; but, given time and thought, I believe there are no limits to the power of perfecting our Humanity, and that the task before us is so to change the forms of our polity as to enable a great change to take place, which is imminent, on our threshold—as, in fact, I have suggested to you in the lectures that lie behind us to-night.

Let me very briefly recall to you the path along which I have tried to lead you. In the first lecture we dealt with the question—Is there a Plan? Then in the second we considered the methods of the Plan, having seen reason enough to accept, as a hypothesis even, that a Plan underlies the whole of the evolution of our world, the whole of the evolution of our system, and probably far, far beyond. In that second lecture we studied the methods, and we found that these might be divided into two parts—the involution of life in matter, and the evolution of matter into a great succession of forms. Looking at the involution, we saw the five stages. The Self, the great Unit, descending into contact with matter, preserves its own essential unity; we may call it the world, or plane, of Unity. Then we saw within that Unity internal divisions arising, so that we had Union; these cohered still together and were encircled as it were by the Unity itself. Descending into a third stage, we found distinct separation; barriers arose, it is the plane of Intellect, the I-hood, the Self-hood, coming downwards in order to shape bodies for his own expression. Then we came to a fourth stage, where attractions and repulsions seemed to be the great new elements unfolding in the life. And lastly, to the denser physical, where the life was most cribbed and cabined, most resisted by external matter—matter almost smothering the life, which had then to subdue matter and make it plastic for its own purposes. Looking at the evolution where the life was to ascend again through the live stages, we found how that showed itself in the formation and the forms of matter. It passed through the lowest of these and made the Mineral Kingdom in the physical world, then onwards to the Vegetable, onwards to the Animal, until it reached the Human form, until Humanity appeared. And we saw that that, so far as we can judge, is the highest form that has yet appeared in this up-climbing of the life, and we noticed in that human form greater and greater refinement and beauty were introduced, and that when the human was, as it were, fixed as the model form, then great internal changes made it more and more responsive to the moulding life within. And we traced that evolution upward, and we found that it had in its way unfolded not only the form of man, but desires and passions and emotions, the second of the upward stages; that it had unfolded mind, the third of the upward stages; and is now on the threshold of the fourth. Looking at it in that way, we came by a sort of compulsion as to what that next stage must be, as we glanced backward at it when the life was occupied in its descent; and we found that we were on the threshold of the plane of Union, where separation was to be largely overcome, where working together was to take the place of working against each other, where we might look forward to a civilisation which should recognise Brotherhood as the law of life, and where gradually we were to see developed all the changes in the polity and the mechanism necessary to make a great co-operative, instead of combative, civilisation. And looking at these great stages, as they came one after another on the stage of Humanity, we noticed that in these there were successive waves, as it were, of civilisation, and that in every case, except the last, there was a Lawgiver moulding the outer civilisation and a Teacher giving a religious form suitable for the proposed outer polity, a religion which should give out the old truths in a new shape, and thus by stage after stage should bring out the various perfections of the ever-unfolding life. But in the fifth we found that there was no lawgiver—there was a religion—no lawgiver to make a polity, because it was the age where individualism especially was to be developed, whether in the individual or the Nation, and hence a religion was given which had in it two great ideals to he successively shown on the world-stage in the great drama. On the one side the evolution of the individual and his value; on the other side the duty of the individual, when he had gained and realised his strength, to turn that strength to service and not to oppression.

And so we came still further onwards, and we were able in this long, long evolution to find, in studying two great divisions of our globe, East and West, that there we came to a great conflict, a conflict first physical, and then a conflict of civilisations and of ideals. And you remember how I pointed out to you that in the East the family was the unit in the Nation, while in the West the individual was the unit in the Nation; that inevitably out of that there came great differences, fundamental differences, in civilisation; for the ideal of the family inevitably develops the sense of corporate life, the sense of the duty of every member of the family to every other, the binding sense of obligation of the various parts of the family; the elders, the contemporaries, and the youngers were bound together in their mutual relationships by this binding law of duty. On the other hand, where the individual was the unit, necessarily the idea of inherent rights arose; and that these rights, as well as the ideal of duty, had both been carried to excess. In the East, where duty was the ideal, there had developed tyranny, the feeling of duty tending to over-submission; while in the West the ideal of rights run to excess led inevitably to conflict, and finally to anarchy. And so it is that along that line of thought, although in very much fuller detail, we find the same fundamental idea as we find here in the rapid sketch made by Sir Michael Sadler, and we realise that we are indeed at the crossway for Humanity to-day; that Humanity has to work out a new form of civilisation, as it has worked out so many forms of civilisation in the past. And so I would say to you that there is every reason for hope and no reason for despair; for man has rebuilt many shattered civilisations on a better basis, and can rebuild the civilisation that lies shattered behind us by the War into a nobler, a more lasting, civilisation *if*—and that *if* is the condition—if he will recognise the laws of Nature as they have not been recognised in the past, the Law of Brotherhood as the basis of civilisation, the Law of Sacrifice as the life and the sustainer of civilisation. And so we come in our study to ask here again, very very briefly, not in detail, how were the older Nations organised? and we may put it, I think, shortly in this form: in those of the East and in Feudal Europe, Mediæval Europe, but especially in the East, the communal feeling was in the ascendant, men felt themselves as a community far more strongly than as individuals; while in the civilisation called by Sir Michael the civilisation of which the essence is Power, there men felt themselves much more as individuals than they realised the bonds of living in a community, the natural feeling which is vital in the future. And looking at it in that way, then we find evolved in the East what is known as the Caste system. That was based entirely on the ideal of Duty; the Duty of the learned to teach; the Duty of the strong to protect; the Duty of the organiser and the distributor of goods to distribute them; and the Duty of the producer to produce. So that you have four great functions coming out in the National life: the Duty of the teacher; the Duty of the protector; the Duty of the organiser and distributor; and the Duty of the producer of wealth. And wherever you find a Nation, these four fundamental duties must always exist; you cannot get rid of them. They are woven into all social, and communal, and National life. And we have to consider how these four functions, the functions of the educator in the widest sense of the term, the functions of the legislator, the functions of the merchant, and the functions of the producer, how these ought to be arranged in a reconstruction of society.

Now the ruin of the caste system was brought about by its becoming a matter of birth only instead of a matter of capacity. There lies the reason why it has become a rigid system which it is found necessary to destroy, if India is to rise to real freedom and real citizenship. And when we look at the less-developed form of caste, the feudal system, we find the same characteristic there fundamentally, the idea of Duty. Privilege was counterbalanced by duty, and there again the birth element came in and led to its destruction eventually. When we look on the later centuries and find the great struggle that takes place in England—we can take England as an example of other western countries—where the individual fights, as it were, for his own hand, there arises the feature of class, and into that from feudalism comes also this element of birth. Personally, although that is a mere detail, and many of you will very likely disagree with it, I think it a very good thing in a Nation that great National Service should be recognised by honour; I believe that that is good, but when it descends to somebody else who has not deserved it, then it becomes an abuse, a danger. If you want to bring in the element of birth you ought to copy the Chinese, who put it on a much more sensible footing. Where a title of honour was given in China, the ancestors were ennobled and not the posterity. Now, that, I submit, is eminently reasonable. They have something or other at least to do with the man who has done great service to the State, as they are his ancestors, and so they may share in the recognition; and the other advantage is that they are not on the physical plane at the moment, and therefore they cannot in any way dishonour the title to the Nation's respect which is bestowed on a particular person. But the moment you run the other way and ennoble the posterity, then you bring in a mischievous element, the element of birth, for it does not follow that his posterity will do well; as a matter of fact, they are sometimes exceedingly unsatisfactory. Then you get a great danger and a great cause of anger, that privilege is given where there is nothing in the individual to deserve it. Privilege gained by duty is one thing; privilege going with an individual life that has no duties imposed on it by the State is a very different thing, and is a source of decay in a civilisation.

Now, looking at it then for a moment from that standpoint, I would ask you: How are we to find out some way in which these functions may be divided? There is only one way that I can think of, and that is by capacities; and the capacities can only be understood, found out, by education, if in education you allow the natural faculties of the child to develop. If in education you insist on a high level of general education and culture, then, and then alone, can you look for social equality. If you take a scientist, if you take a highly educated philosopher, if you take an educated man of any type, provided he is highly educated and cultured, such men or women can meet in perfect social equality, although their avocations may be entirely different. It is not a question of what the man *does,* it is a question of what the man *is*; and education is absolutely necessary before social equality can possibly be gained in any Nation. Hence also education must be prolonged far more than at present is recognised as necessary in modern life. People in modern life are quarrelling over half-timers, over boys and girls who are to earn their own livelihood; but I claim for every child of this Nation the right to develop the whole of his faculties to the utmost extent that those faculties are capable of development, and that implies a long education, not a short or a medium one; it implies not only what I said, that a certain level of education and culture must be common to everyone born into the Nation, but it implies also that as the particular capacities of the young person develop themselves, that is the mark of his place in the National life. What is called vocational education, in the fullest sense of the word, is necessary in order that all the individuals in a Nation may find their appropriate sphere of work; work for which their faculties fit them, and which therefore is an enjoyment in the carrying of it out, and not a drudgery, as it too often is in our own days. Hence I submit that the time for education is the whole period of youth, vocational in the latter part, general in the earlier; and that the education should go as far as the faculties are aided in their development by it—roughly, during the first twenty-one years of life.

Leaving that for a moment—for I shall have just for an instant to return to it in dealing with our Ideal—let me point out to you that the next thing you have to consider is the result in the past of the economic condition of the Nation. You have to start with the question of the holding of land. You have to consider the relationship between labour and capital in the production of wealth. Unless these can be organised on a system of mutual advantage and National contentment, it is impossible, it would be unrighteous, that any civilisation should endure. And so, glancing backward, we find one point of enormous importance as regards the land, and that is, if you take a country like India, land has always been communal property until quite lately. There was no such thing as private ownership of land until after certain arrangements made by the British; until they came there, and brought their own ideas with them, there was no idea that land should ever be held as private property; it was held for use, not for ownership; and the arrangements which were made with other parties in the Village—which was the place where all National wealth was produced—the arrangements made were such that the Village held the land and it was used by the people of the Village. I have not time to go into the details of that. It is an admirable system if you care to look it up. But it came to an end in southern India in 1816. Let me remind you that what we have in India as a Province, you have as a Kingdom. Our Province of Madras has a larger population than England and Wales, and you have to consider that when you are trying to study a very complex civilisation, that varies very much according to the past history of India. But this one may say: everywhere where there were Kings, the King had a right to the produce of part of the land; a part of the land was put aside for the King in exchange for his protection, and cultivated for him, and he was given the produce of the land, not the land. And when he "gave a Village," as you sometimes find, to some successful General, all that the successful General had was the right to the produce of the King's land, but never the ownership of it. Looking at it in that way, you find that the land in India, with the crafts which were carried on in the Village, were enormously remunerative; that these two things, land, labour and capital joined together, were the producers of wealth throughout Indian civilisation. And I may remind you that it admittedly lasted more than five thousand years, and all Indians say immensely longer. I do not want to dwell upon it, but contrast that five thousand years with the four centuries that Sir Michael alleges cover your own civilisation of Power. Not that you need necessarily reproduce it, but that you can learn some great principles from it, and that one great principle is that the land of a Nation is the gift of Nature to the Nation that lives on that land, and not to individuals; and that great principle was recognised not only in the East, but also in Feudal times in Europe, and that is why I classed Feudalism to some extent as Communal, for land in Feudal days, held by the great Nobles, was held under conditions, principally of Military Service, as also in the case even of the Yeoman who held the land under the Feudal System; before that the Village system, which was brought from the East, prevailed, and characterised the times of your greatest freedom, the times of the Anglo-Saxon. But these Feudal nobles bore very heavy duties; they had to bear the whole protection of the Nation, to guard it in Peace and in War, and only by that duty could they keep on holding their land.

Now I know that many great landholders, having been relieved from all duty imposed on them by the State, have imposed duty on themselves by the tradition of their great Order, by their hereditary love for the people who live on the land; and in the cases of men who feel the duty of their past, it has made them the friends and the helpers of their people, and they have discharged, splendidly discharged, their many duties; but they imposed the duties on themselves; it was not the recognition that with the land went duties, and with privilege went responsibility. And so you find many who disregard it and care not for it and are indifferent, and who look on the wealth that comes to them by their ownership as theirs by right, instead of wealth conjoined with duties. And that has been terribly broken up by the War, because, as you know, the great landowners suffer tremendously from wealth taxation, and so they are selling their lands and great houses, and the whole of that side of English civilisation is passing away, with all in it that was beautiful and splendid in its time. It is going down in ruin.

And then, trying to see how the other things are to be changed, I have to remind you that what is called Capital is not only the surplus of labour employed on land or material, but it is also, not as so many people seem idly and foolishly to think, enormous stores of coin, but much more largely credit, so that it vanishes in a most remarkable way. It is not really safe; it is represented by pieces of paper, securities they are called, but they have become "scraps of paper" to a very large extent in regard to the value generally given to them. If you want to see how credit can collapse, look at Russia, where the revolution from which so much was hoped in the beginning has had to allow—despite the ideas of those who led it—Peasant Proprietorship, a new form of ownership, and now is saying that it must have capitalism back again—the result of over-rapid changes where fanatics tried to force a sudden revolution for which the masses of the people were not in any way prepared. And so we come back to this; we find this tremendous difficulty facing us, that the landholders are disappearing; and if you think for a moment of the land-holding as land, you will realise that the land and all that was in the land belonged to them, so that many of them have become enormously wealthy, where coal was discovered, or in other cases iron has been found in their properties, and it is those discoveries that have largely made the enormous differences between wealth and poverty in modern life; not only the wealth of the surface of the land, unjust as that was unless duties were performed in exchange, but everything in the land laid up there by Nature through thousands and millions of years was brought to the surface and became their private property; so some of the enormous fortunes were made of some of the great landholders; and of that you have to think in dealing with reconstruction, because we have now come to the great difficulty that with the disappearance of these great landholders Labour and Capital find themselves face to face. Between them the duel is going on to the destruction of both.

And with that rapid survey of how things are, we have then to realise that great changes should come not by force but by conviction. That is, by great ideals that capture the minds of the people, and so lend to them the enthusiasm by which mighty transformations can be achieved. Do not, because I use the word "Ideal," connect together with it the idea of the unpractical idealist, because I can assure you that if you study history you will find the idealists who stand out from the rest are the most practical people. It is mind and not form that is the creator; and if you could for a moment doubt that an ideal can arouse and transform the characters of men, look back to 1914, and see what the ideals then held up achieved, what an effect they had on the Nations of the world; when in that day when War first broke out, when England held up the ideal of liberty, of faith to her plighted word, and of the protection of a little country unfairly, unrighteously invaded, it was that ideal which sent all the youths of the Universities into the trenches and made them ready to die, not for some sordid reason, not for some hope of personal triumph, but for that great Ideal of Liberty, for which they were willing to perish in order that it might be secure. And that great Ideal rang round the world. It was that that awakened India; that which made India spring to the helping of England; that which drove her soldiers across the sea, coming to a land which was not theirs, to a people whom they did not know, to institutions and customs to which they were utterly alien, and yet which carried them into the trenches, there dying shoulder to shoulder beside your men, believing they fought for Liberty, and therefore willingly throwing their lives away. All that was said over here by your great statesmen who held up those ideals; it was Mr Asquith who taught Indians that a foreign yoke was degradation to a Nation, intolerable, he said, and inconceivable; and his words rang round India. It was that which has largely made Indian unrest, that for which the only possible outcome was to give freedom, as your Parliament happily has begun to give it. Ideals, they are the mightiest things in all the world, the only things that can transform the world, the only things which can change human nature and make the selfish unselfish and the weak strong. And if you think of it for a moment, take it if you will in a much more concrete form than the one I have given, What is the Flag of a Regiment? You may say, only a piece of rag or cloth. Aye, but into that cloth are woven all the memories of the past; into that the common sufferings, the common struggles, the common victories, and also the common defeats ; and that Flag of the regiment has become so much a symbol of its honour to rough men and to poor men, to those of the population here taken into the Army because they could find nothing else which would accept them, that it has transformed their character, so that they are now forbidden to carry their Flag into battle, because it was ever surrounded by heaps of corpses, because they would die rather than let it fall into the enemies' hands. You cannot have a stronger proof of the power of the ideal within the roughest and the most thoughtless of men. It is to these ideals that I trust, to the Ideal of the Future, the creation of that civilisation which I believe the present generation will help in building.

And here I refer again for one moment to Education, only to remind you that the Ideal of the Future for education is in these words which I have already stated; that every child born into our Nation must have the opportunity of developing every capacity he brings with him through the gateway of birth. That, and nothing less than that, is the education that he should have. And I go one step further: I claim that that education shall be free to the child of every citizen; not only the primary education, but the education of the higher schools, of the University itself. For wealth and capacity do not always go together; ability and money are not always found in the same family; and it is capacity to profit by higher education that gives the child or the youth the right to that education.

Now, looking at it in that way, let us consider the three great divisions in a Nation as regards age. I submit that the first twenty-one years should be given to the building of the citizen, that is, to the education of the child, of the youth, and of the young man—including, of course, in the word "man" "woman," as I cannot keep on saying always "he and she"—that is the educational period.

Then, coming to the other extreme of life, old age, in that there should not be bread-winning any more than in the time of youth, for the value of old age to the Nation is experience, knowledge gained by living; and the old men will be the counsellors of the Nation, provided that you have a number also of the mature, of the young, in order that the future may be considered as well as the past.

And the middle period of life, from twenty-one onwards to whatever you make your beginning of old age—as it differs much with different people,—whatever that time may be, the bread-winning period of life should be always between those two limits. The duty of the young is to study to be good citizens. The duty of the mature is to live the life of the citizen, discharging every duty faithfully. The duty of old age is to be of any service they can to the Nation, in which they have been educated, in which they have served.

And so you begin to realise that in this Nation you will have to begin to reorganise it into the great functions; and that, I think, is what Sir Michael means when he speaks about these three things which sustained the harmonious life of Christendom; he calls them the Priesthood, the Empire, and the University. For "Priesthood" I would like to substitute the Spiritual and Intellectual Teachers of the Nation. The word "Priest" I have no objection to, but it is as true of science as it is true of religion—except in the sense that in religion it is used for dealing with the greater verities of human life and emotions and mentality, leading those onwards along a spiritual path, while in science the Priest of science is the Interpreter of Nature here, the Nature which surrounds us with its countless phenomena. And I submit you must have the class from which you can take your Priest, or, if you prefer it, the class which is the Teacher of the Nation in every line of thought and life. It would include the scientist and the doctor, the philosopher and the metaphysician, the whole of the learned men, the thinkers, and the artists of the Nation, who come under this great head ; for they are really the educators of the people, and not only the teachers of the schools, of the colleges, and of the universities. And this class is necessary for the Nation's advance and prosperity. It does not need great wealth; it needs great knowledge and wisdom. And their duty is helping others to share in that which their intellect has discovered and formulated to the world and thus enlightened it. Intellect illuminated by the Spirit is the guide of the spiritual life of the people, and without that spiritual life no civilisation will endure; for material ideals alone can never uplift a Nation to an enduring life; you must have the ideal of the spiritual before you, and that means the Oneness of the Whole.

And just as you must have your educative class, so you must have your Statesmen and your Legislature and your Army and your Navy and your Police— although I hope the functions of the three last will become very much lighter as the duties of the Teachers are more fully and more justly discharged. And on that I venture to differ from a very eminent man when he said it was not the job of the teachers of religion to interfere in the other departments of life, like labour, industry, the relations of mercantile bodies, politics, and the rest. There is no department of human life into which religion should not enter and spiritualise that department. The great duty of the teaching class in all its phases, whether of science or of religion, was, and is, to spiritualise each department. Of politics, so that they may be the politics of noble and upright men, and no excuses be made for political expedients to cover falsity, or perjury, or wrong. To spiritualise all mercantile relationships, so that a merchant should not do in his mercantile capacity what he would not do to his friend or to his brother. To spiritualise labour, so that the man who produces may fill his vocation in the Nation, and realise that to labour honourably, truthfully, well, is as spiritual a vocation as that of any priest or minister of religion can be. Only in that way shall we learn either the Law of Brotherhood or the Law of Sacrifice; for every vocation in a Nation is honourable, provided it is honourably done and carried out uprightly and righteously.

Now, what signs are there in our world of to-day in this direction? There is certainly a tendency towards Union. You will remember I spoke of Union as on the threshold—in the higher sense I was then thinking of it; and that tendency is everywhere manifest. And if you are going to deal with those two great powers, Capital and Labour, thousands struggling for victory, you will find this principle is coming in on both sides—unions of workmen and unions of capitalists. With regard to the former, I should like to make one remark. You must all realise that in the great struggles of the day it is not the question of wage which is really at the root of the struggle of Labour. Of that for which labour is working, wage is only the symbol. What they are working for is a higher human life, so that they may know, so that they may share, some of those things which to you and to me are the commonplaces of life, but in which they have no share to-day. It is not human life simply to labour, and to sleep in order to labour again. Human life is something grander, and nobler, and greater than that. It is Art as much as Toil, for it has Beauty as its manifestation. It has hope of the future in Knowledge and in Wisdom. It has delight in the present by all the ennobling enjoyments that Art and that Culture make possible for man. And so I would say that every man in a Nation has that life as a right, no matter what the avocation his hands or his brain may lead him to follow. And in the Trade Union that is felt very deeply. And one point I would venture to recall, that I mentioned last week, the idea that the most skilled mechanic is not to work his best, because if he does a weaker and less-skilled workman will not be able to get a decent living. Men of great ability and skill and energy will not produce what they can, and can easily, do—not because they want to limit production, but because they feel the weak man is their brother. And so they will not outrace him, because brothers must stand side by side. And in that recognition there is a splendour of spiritual insight which is hidden entirely by the form in which that desire clothes itself in putting itself forth to the world. When I said lately in this hall that the axiom of the present civilisation was that the best man should WIN, but that the axiom of the future was that the best man should SERVE, the whole hall rang with plaudits. That is a fundamental truth, and with whatever clumsiness in endeavouring to reach it the rule to which I alluded has been carried out, there is in it that Law of Brotherhood, as recognised, not unfortunately in the whole Nation, but within a single unit. It is the germ of the better realisation that strength is meant for service and not for going faster or better than another man—the realisation of the great Law of Brotherhood. You would not outrace your brother. That is the thought that underlies what I called a mischievous expression, because it enfeebles the Nation; and that is eminently wrong.

But all these things are passing, and will be grown out of. What it is desirable now to recognise is that you must go onward into a life in which the motive is a common motive, and in which work is for the common good; in which we want to help each other, and not to trample each other down. That is the Union into which we must inevitably pass. It is the next stage in evolution, and if it is not accepted willingly, then it will come by destruction, for that which is against Nature cannot endure.

Now of Great Britain, I ask: What is her place in the Plan? Great Britain has a possibility before her, and a power of accomplishing that possibility, which are not so great in any other Nation in the world. I will tell you exactly what I mean. When I was here in 1919 it was just in the crash of the Russian Revolution, and I ventured to say to a great body of Trade Unionists and working men that Britain was the one country in the world, I believed, where by training and self-discipline and the power of combination in the unions, and the learning in the unions of discipline, there was good hope that this tremendous transformation might be made without revolution or violence. Things are not as hopeful to-day as they were then; and largely because the sense of duty, and of discipline and loyalty to leaders is lacking; these things have broken down very much amongst those who were the most splendid examples of them a few years ago; and that because a class is taking the place of the Nation and the power of the class—what they are pleased to call

44

the dictation of the proletariat—is striving to compel the Nation. There is no class, autocratic or democratic or proletariat or monarchic, that has the right to dictate to the Nation and say what it should do. It is not because they are many that they have the right to kill Liberty. Not because they are strong and can starve the Nation into submission have they the right to tyrannise. I protested against it when employers tried to starve the workmen into breaking unionism; and I protest against it as much to-day, when the strong by numbers try to starve the country, because they are engaged in quarrels with their employers. I believe it is possible that these dangers can be overcome, and I want to put to you as my last point that the tendencies everywhere are not only towards Union within the Nation, but of Union of larger and larger Nations as we go on in evolution. In the past those larger Unions have always been made by military force, by power, by trampling on the weaker Nations and incorporating them with the stronger by annexation of other peoples' countries. That they call annexation rather than robbery, because it is a prettier word and covers over what really has occurred. They have been made by aggressive war, which is murder on a vaster scale, which is the outcome of hatred, and therefore destructive and demoralising; and by diplomacy, which is too often only a many-syllabled word for untruth and intrigue.

Now Britain has the opportunity to make a mighty Empire—Empire I call it for a moment, for its name has been Empire hitherto; and the great point which was decided by the Maker of the Plan in the last war was, that two Empires, symbolising two great principles, should be flung together in the clash of war. And the one principle was the principle of autocracy and military power, and there was a splendid, highly organised army to rule the world by the imposition of power. And the other principle was a loosely knit kind of Empire, with, as the other side called it, "a contemptible little army," very small, a thing to be walked over by the great military power, and the loosely knit Empire was to be rent in pieces in the clash of war. But to the world's wonder it went the other way, and that loosely knit Empire became more and more closely knit together as the war went on, and grew stronger and stronger, and learned to organise power for war, and took many steps onward which now they are trying to undo. They nationalised the railways because they wanted to carry their soldiers, their munitions, and their supplies of every sort; and now it is said that State management does not pay, because all that was done free, without payment. The soldiers paid nothing, and the State paid nothing for them; and then they say State management is so very expensive. But you organised for war, because without it you would have perished; and as you organised for war, cannot you organise for peace in order that your people shall be happy? If you organised for war against soldiers, cannot you organise against poverty and ignorance and misery, and turn the whole power of the State in order that the nation shall be happy and prosperous and contented? The same ability which organised for war can organise for peace. The same sacrifice that organised for war can also organise for peace. Britain's opportunity is hers, because all round the world there are Free Nations that have sprung from her, that you call the Self-Governing Dominions, and other lands that have been acquired largely by the help of their own people, and which you call Dependencies or Colonies; they, all that huge possibility of all those varied Nations, not only of white people but of coloured, not only of western Nations but of eastern, not only of Europe but of Asia, are awaiting federation. Think what it means if, for the first time in the world, a Power as strong as you admittedly are to-day, instead of relying on strength, tries to seek for and to do justice. Instead of trying who can arm the most, try who can serve the best. Instead of trying to tyrannise over others, open to them the gates of Freedom, and say to all the Nations that make up this great Empire: "Come and form with us not an Empire, but a great Commonwealth of Free Nations; not a white Commonwealth, but a Commonwealth into which men of every race, of every colour, of every ancestry, of every creed, of every tradition and custom, shall come willingly as free members." Ah I If Britain can do that, then she will do her part in the Great Plan. That is her place; that is her opportunity. No other Nation with dominions so widespread and so varied can build up that mighty Commonwealth of Brotherhood, of all the races of every faith, of every colour, of every line of thought. Have you the strength to do it? I believe you have. Have you the love to do it? I hope you have.

That is your place in the Plan; take it or leave it. It is your decision, your right to say what you will do. But if you can do it, if you will do it, if you will encourage Freedom and not try to hold her back, if you will welcome her everywhere where your power extends; if you will help, strengthen, inspire, lead, but let the Nations take their Freedom and be your brothers and not your subjects—then you will do more than make a great Federation, then you will do more than build a mighty Commonwealth; you will build a Model, which the world shall copy; you will build a Temple, which shall become the model for the Temple of Humanity; within your own power you will make Freedom extend everywhere over your Dominions, and thus set an example that other Nations shall follow; for you will never reach true Internationalism until the Nations have recognised their Brotherhood, and have willingly joined together in bonds of Love, of Amity, and of Freedom.

www.ingramcontent.com/pod-product-compliance
Lightning Source LLC
Chambersburg PA
CBHW070830100426
42813CB00003B/555